PELICAN BOOKS

Biological Ideas in Politics

W. J. M. Mackenzie was born in 1909 in Edinburgh and educated at Balliol College, Oxford, where he was a classical scholar, and Edinburgh University, where he took a law degree. At Oxford he taught classics from 1933 to 1936 and politics from 1936 to 1948, apart from the war, when he served for five years as a civil servant with the Air Staff and with the Joint Staff Mission in Washington. In 1949 he became Professor of Government at Manchester University, and in 1966 he was appointed to a chair in the Department of Politics at Glasgow University and is now Professor Emeritus. From 1952 to 1960 he was an adviser on East African constitutional development, and since 1959 he has been an adviser on the development of English regional and local government. He was awarded the C.B.E. in 1963 and was elected Fellow of the British Academy in 1968.

With J. W. Grove, Professor Mackenzie has written *Central Administration in Britain* (1957). He has also written *Free Elections* (1958), *The Study of Political Science Today* (1972), *Politics and Social Science* (Penguin, 1967), *Power, Violence, Decision* (Penguin, 1975), *Political Identity* (Penguin, 1978) and, with K. Robinson, he has edited *Five Elections in Africa* (1959).

W. J. M. MACKENZIE

Biological Ideas in Politics

An essay on political adaptivity

PENGUIN BOOKS

Penguin Books Ltd, Harmondsworth, Middlesex, England
Penguin Books, 625 Madison Avenue, New York, New York 10022, U.S.A.
Penguin Books Australia Ltd, Ringwood, Victoria, Australia
Penguin Books Canada Ltd, 2801 John Street, Markham, Ontario, Canada L3R 1B4
Penguin Books (N.Z.) Ltd, 182–190 Wairau Road, Auckland 10, New Zealand

—

First published in Penguin Books 1978

—

Copyright © W. J. M. Mackenzie, 1978
All rights reserved

—

Made and printed in Great Britain by
Cox & Wyman Ltd, London, Reading and Fakenham
Set in Intertype Times

Tito Lucretio Caro
Votum Solvit
Lubens Merito

W.J.M.M.

Contents

In the animal kingdom the rule is, eat or be eaten;
in the human kingdom, define or be defined.

Thomas Szasz, *The Second Sin*,
Routledge & Kegan Paul, 1973

Preface

THIS book is based on the Sir Douglas Robb lectures which I was invited to give at the University of Auckland in August 1975. It was a great honour to be invited to join in commemorating a great man, one of many sons of Scottish families who helped to build New Zealand. It was also a great pleasure to visit New Zealand, to see so much of the country, and to enjoy New Zealand hospitality.

I suppose that Scots, rugby footballers, political scientists, naturalists, mountaineers, foresters and farmers (I can marginally claim a toe-hold in each of these categories) idealize New Zealand a little too much. But only a little: to many strangers New Zealand is a mythological place – the crossing of the mountains in Samuel Butler's *Erewhon*; Macaulay's image of the 'traveller from New Zealand, in the midst of a vast solitude, taking his stand on a broken arch of London Bridge, to sketch the ruins of St Paul's'; John Wyndham's vision of New Zealand in his novel *The Chrysalids*,[1] as the guardian of the future in a world scorched by nuclear catastrophe; indeed, McNeish's myth of the shepherd Mackenzie and his dog,[2] and the heritage of Maori myth, which has become the common property of all in New Zealand – the greatest islands in the South Pacific.

I must also thank the Politics and Biology group of the International Political Science Association and its chairman, Professor Al Somit of the State University of New York at Buffalo, associates in this intellectual enterprise; and I owe thanks in particular to the Chancellor and Vice-Chancellor of the University of Auckland; to Professor Bob Chapman and the staff of the Political Studies Department; to the Registrar,

1. Penguin, 1958.
2. James McNeish, *The Mackenzie Affair*, Auckland, 1972, and his novel, *Mackenzie*, Hodder & Stoughton, 1970.

Mr D. W. Pullar and his staff; to the audiences who supported me; and to the ladies, in Auckland and Glasgow, who coped with my crabbed handwriting and much amended drafts.

1

Introduction

'Man is an unspecialized animal. His body, except for his enormous brain case, is primitive. He can't dig; he can't run very fast; he can't fly. But he can eat anything and he can stay alive where a goat would starve, a lizard would fry, a bird freeze. Instead of special adaptations he has general adaptability.' Robert Heinlein, *Beyond This Horizon*, Panther Books, 1967, pp. 34–5

IT is just about forty years since I became officially 'a political scientist', that is to say, I was appointed to a post which involved teaching and writing 'political science' – not constitutional law nor political history nor political philosophy nor political economy, certainly not psychology or sociology – but 'political science'. There seems to be a general consensus that I have been busy at it (or at least harmlessly idle) for more than a generation. But what have I been doing?

There are two words here, 'political' and 'science', both of them trailing clouds of ambiguity and multiple reference. 'Political' is the easier of the two. I was interested in 'politics' but was not to practise but to teach; not to 'teach politics' as if I were teaching golf or love-making, but to teach *about* politics. Pupils would turn up, it was supposed, who already had an interest in politics, or might be conscripted unsuspecting because some authority had enacted that they should be taught about politics, and that they should, if possible, be enticed into making at least a decent show of interest. But what is 'politics'? Every academic will recognize a question so phrased. It is a 'meta' question, a question asking not for a first-level but for a second-level answer. 'What is the difference between an elephant and a letterbox?' 'You give up?' 'Well, I wouldn't send *you* to post a letter.' The form of the question postulates that we recognize politics when we see it, but that we are not certain how to specify it in words or other inter-personal symbols. Will it turn out to be like trying to explain the colour scarlet to a man born blind? The classic answer to that question is that 'scarlet is like the sound of a trumpet'; we can attempt to illuminate by metaphor and analogy. Or we can attempt to illuminate, ostensively, by pointing to examples: that, and that, and that, are cases of politics. But no professional pedant can be expected to stop there; the urge to define a word is an urge to control and manage the word, and also the implications of the word, and we pedants have been at this game since the word politics first cropped up in Western languages about a hundred generations ago.

So far so good; there is a word 'politics', a tradition of politics, a tradition of discourse about politics. But what about 'science'? The story is rather similar even though politics is a Greek word and science is a Latin word. However, the word in Latin came to refer to a Greek word, *episteme*, which was distinguished fairly consistently both from 'recognition' of things seen, heard, smelt, tasted or touched, and from the patiently acquired skill of the specialized craftsman, his *techne*. *Scientia* must be systematic and communicable knowledge, inter-personal and objective in the sense that for everyone everywhere $2 + 2 = 4$. That is the extreme case; but *scientia* tends towards symbolic forms which by-pass the ambiguities of natural language.

I rather think that in German *Wissenschaft*, in French *science*, in Italian *scienza* have retained a wide reference to that long search for inter-personal truth. And the English word 'science' had the same implications up to about the 1850s. But there then came into being the British Association for the Advancement of Science, and there followed (primarily in the 1870s) a so-called confrontation between religion and science; between Bishop Wilberforce ('Soapy Sam') and the first of the Huxley dynasty, the formidable Professor T. H. Huxley: 'Is Man an Angel or an Ape?';[1] and so on.

The debate died away but the semantic shift has remained. In

1. For a good account see Cyril Bibby, *Scientist Extraordinary: The Life and Scientific Works of Thomas Henry Huxley, 1825–1895*, Pergamon, 1972.

English, and specifically in American English, the words 'science' and 'scientific' have been limited in some way, still very hard to define, to something less than the whole universe of organized knowledge. For instance, the work of Karl Marx is certainly in the old sense *wissenschaftlich*; but certainly it is not, in the new 'anglo-saxon' sense, 'scientific'.

Hence many misunderstandings, in which I had never expected to become involved. I brought to 'political science' a broad though shallow knowledge of constitutional law, international law, political history and political philosophy; and the Second World War came before I could reach a decent show of 'systematic understanding' of the politics of the 1930s which drove all of us together into that desperate situation. During the war I had a privileged (and not too dangerous) view of decision-making at high levels. In particular, I had a fairly close relation to such eminent scientists as Lindemann, Tizard, and Watson-Watt, and found them neither less nor more rational, neither less nor more human than Air Marshals, top civil servants and top politicians. They lay well within the range of my cloistered academic experience. Indeed Francis Cornford's *Microcosmographia Academica*, his satire on Cambridge University politics before 1914, was favourite reading for the more sophisticated gamesters, such as Air Chief Marshal Wilfred Freeman, of the Ministry of Aircraft Production, and Sir William Farren of Farnborough, Avro and Hawker Siddeley. My range of vision never included a direct view of anything worse than the bombing of London but it was stretched to the limits of imagination by the commission to write from official sources of British relations with resistance movements in Europe during the Second World War. Yet there was nothing there that was not in Thucydides' history of the Peloponnesian war in the fifth century B.C.

So I emerged from an old tradition to find myself teaching political *science* in a new sense. But that needs further explanation. Sir Ernest Barker, in his last big book, *Principles of Social and Political Theory*, writes with devotion of 'my master Aristotle'. The book was published in 1951, when Barker was seventy-seven, and it belongs in a sense to the last great period

13

of self-confident English writing about politics, the twenty years or so before 1914. We were still, in the 1930s, dominated by the constitutional text-books of that period; some of the brilliant young men were then still with us – Ernest Barker, Sandy Lindsay; H. J. Laski – and we still used as an introductory text Graham Wallas on *Human Nature in Politics*, published in 1908. I think we should almost all have followed Barker in acknowledging 'our master Aristotle', but each of us understood Aristotle differently, as metaphysician and theologian, as ethical teacher, as architect of constitutions, as natural scientist – many different Aristotles and yet one man, *the* political scientist.

By 1945 that period was gone at last and the mould was broken. There were of course many factors involved, and I mention only two. One of them was symbolized by the title of Lionel Robbins's very influential book, *The Name and Nature of Economic Science*, first published in 1932. 'We have seen that [Economic Science] provides, within its own structure of generalizations, no norms which are binding in practice. It is incapable of deciding as between the desirability of different ends. It is fundamentally distinct from Ethics' (2nd edn, p. 152). 'Economics' (no longer 'political economy') was then the leader among the social sciences in Britain, and we were obliged to listen when leading economists preached the scientific obligation to make a clean cut between fact and value. We did not necessarily obey, nor did all economists; but we could not contract out of the debate.

The other factor was the new predominance of America in the social sciences, and in political science in particular. This was partly a matter of scale and partly a matter of professional organization. In 1936 I joined the American Political Science Association and subscribed to its journal, basically because there was nothing else to join and no other specialist periodical to read; partly it was because the U.S.A. had a relatively short war and conducted it in a way which gave a professional boost to social scientists, perhaps to behavioural psychologists in particular. Two books that had to be digested were Samuel Stouffer, *The American Soldier*, published in 1949, and the

Lazarsfeld and Berelson book on the Presidential election of 1944, *The People's Choice*, published in 1944.[1] To this one must add the erratic but always stimulating influence of Harold Lasswell, a native American empiricist, a student of the old Chicago School and yet open to the charms of psychoanalysis; and then the irruption into America of Central European vocabulary and debate We in England had never heard of Max Weber, of *wertfrei*, of *Politik als Beruf*, or of the problems of transposing these German words into 'anglo-saxon'. Still less had we heard of 'the Frankfurt School' and the conceptual origins of T. W. Adorno's massive German/Jewish/American project on *The Authoritarian Personality*, published eventually in 1950.[2]

We had to learn; but meanwhile we christened ourselves 'The Political *Studies* Association' and took modest pride in the Nuffield College electoral 'studies'.

Speaking for myself alone, I did not find it easy, partly because American internal controversy was massive and confused, though flashes of fire came occasionally from the dark clouds; it took me years to realize that the so-called 'behavioural controversy' included two elements intricately confused. One of them was that of Germanic *Wissenschaft*, of over-arching general theory, the comprehensive and meticulously dove-tailed specification of a *Weltanschauung*, to which each empirical observation is of necessity related. The other was the native American tradition of piecemeal empirical science and 'piecemeal social engineering'. The latter phrase we owe to Sir Karl Popper of Vienna, who built a bridge between pragmatism and *Postivismus*; it is he whom we know best in England (and of course also in New Zealand where he wrote *The Open Society and its Enemies*); but, in America, American analysts of natural science have been even more influential than Popper.

Elsewhere, I have written a certain amount, very diffidently, about over-arching theory and its intricate pedigree;[3] the theme of this book arises out of the other branch of speculation, the

1. With Helen Gaudet, Columbia U.P.
2. Harper & Row, New York.
3. *Politics and Social Science*, Penguin, 1967, ch. 8.

assimilation by political science of the techniques and criteria of the natural sciences.

It is this branch of the argument that I propose to follow here, on the Socratic principle of following the *logos* wherever it may lead.[1] It led me, all innocent, into some unexpected places, and perhaps this is the place for a brief summary.

Invited to explore the analogy of the natural sciences, for various reasons I chose biology, and this led me at once to the scientific study of man as part of nature, and to the existence of a modern scientific orthodoxy about how we got here and what sort of animal we are. All animals are in some sense 'social' and social behaviour is a part of their genetic inheritance. But social behaviour is also learnt, more or less perfectly, and it is to that extent plastic. Man is socially the most plastic of all animals and owes his biological success above all to his social adaptivity.

And from talking social adaptivity it is a short step to talking politics.

So I used this analogy in a seminar paper, stressing that it was to be used only as an analogy, and that the biologists do not say that man is *only* an animal.[2] But these apotropaic gestures proved to be quite futile, and what seemed to me to be a scientific orthodoxy at once attracted very sharp critics from various different quarters. I try in chapter three to state these criticisms and to meet them or evade them. And perhaps evasion is the right tactic because, while these speculations were evolving in my mind, social biology and ecology suddenly became political in a way which I had never anticipated, nor had the scientists. Towards the end of the 1960s it became a commonplace, a well advertised and saleable commonplace, that man had been too successful as an animal; that by his ever-accelerating growth in numbers and skills he threatened his environment and therefore (as the laws of population ecology

1. *Political Identity*, Penguin, 1978.

2. 'Whatever we may think or believe about man must be consistent with what we know about evolution and man's history.' Angus Martin, *The Last Generation: The End of Survival?*, Fontana/Collins, 1975, p. 8, quoting R. D. Alexander, 'The Search for an Evolutionary Philosophy of Man', Proceedings of the Royal Society of Victoria, 84, 1971, pp. 99–120.

require) his own future as a species. Hence the academic and also political controversy over limits of growth which I discuss quite briefly and superficially in chapter four.

Given the ecumenical acceptance of this argument, at least as a framework for controversy, I feel entitled in the last chapter to return to the analogy of chapter two. Man by his biological success has run (as do all successful populations) into the problems of exponential growth. He will get out of them only by social adaptivity; in the modern world that means by the creation of relevant institutions, and of myths and *mores* that can sustain them. And I end with some rambling discussion of Britain as an adaptive political system, and of the application of the analogy to the politics of all mankind.

2

The Natural History of Man: An Orthodoxy

'This, I reflected, is God showing what men are, to let them see they are no better than the beasts. For man's fate is a beast's fate, one fate befalls them both; as the one dies so the other dies, the same breath is in them all.' 3 Ecclesiastes 18: 19 (Moffat's translation)

THERE was, I can now see, a certain confusion in my approach, a confusion which is in fact very common. Various accidents led me to pick biology as the relevant science. In the days when the way to competitive success still led through Latin and Greek my scientific and mathematical education was neglected. But a couple of intelligent and perceptive schoolmasters had set me to work when I was a schoolboy of leisure (it must have been some time in 1926 or 1927) to demonstrate a very beautiful and quite misleading physical model of Niels Bohr's atom (then the latest); my father was something of a field naturalist and introduced me at an early age to the book by the banker Eliot Howard on *Territory in Bird Life* (published in 1920),[1] from which so much has followed; at Balliol in the late 1920s I worked quite hard, under Cyril Bailey's guidance, on Lucretius' Latin poem, 'On the Nature of Things', which compels one to consider the conceptual relation between ancient and modern science;[2] and Magdalen in the 1930s included a most congenial group of young scientists, among them James Griffiths and Pat Johnson (physics), John Eccles (physiology), John Young, Peter Medawar (biology), Brian Maegraith (tropical medicine), Eric Moullin (electrical engineering). I had no cause to be frightened of scientists but, if one were to look for manageable and comprehensible science on which to build

1. John Murray.
2. There has just appeared a new translation by C. H. Sisson, Carcanet New Press, Manchester, 1976, which conveys marvellously the power and personality of the poem.

one's own understanding, physics was mathematically too hard, biology more attractive. The book by Walter Bagehot called *Physics and Politics* (1872) is really about biology and politics – one of Bagehot's weaker books, but full of promising lines of thought, as was also Graham Wallas's book on *Human Nature in Politics* (1908). Besides, biology is interesting and exciting to read; I am too lazy to be a field naturalist, too clumsy to be an experimentalist, but the procedures of biology are readily intelligible, and (above all) one can, in the case of biology, see quite readily how complex statistical operations fit into the whole picture of a science.

My thought was that if one is to play with the idea of a natural science of politics, it must be 'end-on' to biology, or perhaps even be a part of biology. Man is an animal; as Aristotle put it, he is a political animal. The natural history of man has made enormous and exciting steps in the last twenty years; one of its main themes is that man conquered the world because he excelled all other animals in social adaptivity.

I can now see that I was confusing three different ways of applying any natural science, and biology in particular, in any field of social science. The first is to treat the field of biology as analogous to the field of society. Probably every language uses biological metaphors in talk about society. These may be made explicit poetically in myths and fables; they may be abstracted to form symbolic models, sometimes even quantifiable, as in the relationship between the models of economics and those of ecology. I have written at some length recently about 'the biological metaphor',[1] and I shall not re-open that discussion here, except to say that the metaphor is irresistible and adds life (there goes that metaphor again) to political rhetoric at many levels – but watch for it.

The second thing is to say to oneself – 'that is a very good and profitable science, let us copy its methods' – and this can happen unconsciously, or at least naïvely, as is easily seen when someone trained to think as a biologist or as an engineer, or in some other powerful discipline, begins to think methodically about human society. I have no claim at all to explain the methods of

1. *Power, Violence, Decision*, Penguin, 1975, ch. 4.

biology but perhaps it is worth saying that one learns fairly quickly to think of the biological sciences, or the life sciences, in the plural, that is to say, there is a single focus, life, a puzzle which we seek to understand, but there are many techniques and methods. There is a range of scale, from that of the ecology of planet earth to that of molecular chemistry; there is a range of method – library study, field study, laboratory work; there are various different kinds of output, such as taxonomy, or evolutionary theory, or mathematical modelling. There is not much in this that we can use or imitate directly, but it may help us to cultivate humility and patience.

The third thing is to treat man as, in some sense, the subject of biology, the natural history of man as 'end-on' to the study of other forms of life.[1] I use the words 'political adaptivity' as a catch-phrase or ticket for the appeal to biological science in that sense, and, in the present discussion, I am reverting to an old paradox that man is, and is not, part of nature. Man's cell biology, man's digestive system, man's reproductive system, and so on, must be regarded as parts of nature; yet there are characteristics of man for which no analogies or antecedents have yet been found in nature.

But I emphasize the word 'yet' because I want first to take science on its own terms, and simply to put out a version of the natural history of man in a deadpan way: it is not at all an authoritative version, and I expect biologists to put me right about its scientific basis. But it is enough for my argument if I can sustain that this is orthodox science and that even its paradoxes can be handled on the basis of natural science.

The most important paradox is that one has to begin like the Book of Genesis: 'In the beginning God created the heaven and the earth. And the earth was without form, and void; and darkness was upon the face of the deep: and the Spirit of God moved upon the face of the waters.'[2]

I have patiently read what the pundits say to the public about the rival theories of the creation of this universe, the 'big bang'

1. Cf. the postscript (and peroration) of Michael Ruse, *The Philosophy of Biology*, Hutchinson, 1973.
2. I Genesis 1: 2.

and the 'steady state', and so far as I can see neither of them is truly about creation: the fundamental stuff, whatever it was – it seems to be usual now to call it mass/energy – was there all the time, and *must* have been there all the time, because one cannot have a science about something coming out of nothing. Science is about transformations, not about creation.

So wrote Lucretius, poet and scientist, in the time of Julius Caesar,[1] and attempts have been made ever since to evade the resultant paradoxes, to say that the dimension of time is by its very nature creative, or that there are 'emergent qualities', embodied in systematic wholes, entities not reducible to their components, or that there exist individual things the individuality of which escapes the net of science. But one comes back to the flat, tedious, practical rule which Lucretius borrowed from the Greek atomists – *de nilo nil fit* ('out of nothing, nothing'): if your experiments appear to contradict it you had better think again.

At the time when I was writing this, a political science student inflicted on me an essay which dragged into a politics question about natural rights St Thomas Aquinas' version of the five rational arguments for the existence of God. The language at first seemed very peculiar and irrelevant to the question set; but, on reflection, I liked it. I doubt whether the big bang and steady state have improved on Genesis and on St Thomas, except in one respect.

The exception is that, however the thing was set spinning in the first place, it is a postulate of scientific investigation that once the celestial machine was set going it would run without special intervention until the end of time. It is a postulate of natural religion, on the other hand, throughout mankind, that special interventions happen all the time and have their own rules, different from the rules of technical practice but equally valid. The development of science has now narrowed the scope for intervention to the study of a number of crises at which

1. 'To shatter the dark towers of superstition we need, not sunlight and the bright shafts of day, but observation of nature and a rational account of it. The first principle of my account is this: nothing is ever created miraculously out of nothing.' Lucretius I, 146–50 (my own free translation).

there appears to be a break in continuity; these are quite familiar – the transition from matter to life, the transition from ape to man, the transition from man the wandering scavenger to man the master and destroyer of nature. The thesis of Jacques Monod[1] and other unflinching scientists is that, between these crises, exploration is now a matter of what Kuhn[2] calls 'normal science', just as normal as the development of new drugs or new jet engines, and that for each crisis there now exists a set of tools and procedures which will soon break the paradox and re-establish continuity.

At one time life seemed as paradoxical as creation; to be in fact a second creation. In my first approach to philosophy[3] the fashion was still in favour of Henri Bergson and *L'Evolution Créatrice* (1907),[4] the most massive exploration of the theme that matter and life are eternally different, that matter is dead and unchanging, that life, *l'elan vital*, creates continually what is radically new. There were many much cruder versions of vitalism, as it was called; all of them now seem to be dead.

The gap between matter and life now seems to be closing from both sides. On the one hand, the talk is of physical and chemical evolution, the process by which, both conceptually and through actual time, more complex atoms arise from simpler atoms, more complex molecules from simpler molecules. Clearly, physical scientists are highly romantic and very competitive and we need not believe all we read in the journals of popular science; but they seem very confident that there are laws of the

1. *Le hasard et la nécessité: essai sur la philosophie naturelle de la biologie moderne*, Seuil, Paris, 1970. Monod's title refers directly to the tradition of Democritus, to which Lucretius belonged, that all things are governed by *tyché* and *anangké* (chance and necessity), metaphysical, even mythological, words which have in modern science been given scientific and mathematical meanings.

2. *The Structure of Scientific Revolutions*, Chicago U.P., 1962.

3. This was at Balliol about 1930. The then Master, A. D. Lindsay, had published a book about Bergson in 1911 and, of course, H. G. Wells and Bernard Shaw had both sucked in ideas from that *milieu*, to be used as dramatic myths.

4. Alcan, Paris, 34th edn., 1929, p. 95.

evolution of matter and that these can be found and stated.[1]

The gap is being closed from the other side partly by methods of the same kind, which have pushed biochemistry down to the level of the huge molecules of *The Double Helix*,[2] the chemical level of biological control, innovation and selection. But there is also a different trick, that of defining life or defining it away. Here my primary sources[3] have been Schrödinger, van Bertalanffy, Monod, J. Z. Young, Darlington; and, after a time, I began to think that there was something odd about the character of the question. My suspicion was confirmed when I found that the old *Encyclopaedia Britannica* (the 1961 edition) had no article at all on this thing called 'life'. The new edition (1974) says in its 'Micropaedia' simply that 'life is a phenomenon almost impossible to define or explain in all its varying aspects'. The 'Macropaedia' says (with equal simplicity) 'a great deal is known about life', and goes on to thirty-four columns of detail.

The implication, I am sure, is that the scientists cannot yet give us the definition we want. There are various sorts of definition that will not satisfy us: stipulative definition, operational definition, ostensive definition, for example. What we want might be called a 'cook-book' definition, a prescription for creating life out of non-life – and that no one will give us.

Instead, we are still offered negatives, what life is not. It is argued, for instance, that life is not a 'thing', in either of two recognized sources of the word. On the one hand, the fundamental creed of physical science includes the Second Law of

1. Melvin Calvin, *Chemical Evolution*, Clarendon Press, 1969.

2. James D. Watson, Weidenfeld & Nicolson, 1968.

3. E. Schrödinger, *What is Life? The Physical Aspect of the Living Cell*, Cambridge U.P., 1944; *Mind and Matter*, Cambridge U.P., 1958.

L. von Bertalanffy, *Problems of Life: An Evaluation of Modern Biological Thought* (in German, 1949), English trans. Watts, London, 1952; *General System Theory: Foundations, Development, Applications*, Braziller, New York, 1967; *Robots, Men and Minds: Psychology in the Modern World*, Braziller, 1967.

J. Z. Young, *An Introduction to the Study of Man*, Clarendon Press, 1971.

C. D. Darlington, *The Evolution of Man and Society*, Allen & Unwin, 1969.

Thermodynamics, the one which Lord Snow expects all cultured persons to understand.[1] It has indeed become the basis of various flaming metaphors: it is Time's Arrow, it is the heat death of the universe, it is the slide of all things towards disorder. But, says a convenient popular text, 'disorder is a tricky fellow to pin down ... Disorder is not an absolute concept; rather it is relative and has meaning only in context.'[2] And the authors give various definitions and various illustrations, including the favourite one, that you cannot unboil a kettle. You can reverse the visual and auditory record of a kettle boiling by reversing the run of photographic film and tape through a projector; but you cannot recapture the molecules of water which became steam. Even more obviously, you can run backwards the film of a pole-vault or a cricket shot, but the vaulter cannot unvault, the off-drive cannot be undriven. Time will not 'run back, and fetch the age of gold'.

More strictly, these things are not physically impossible; merely, they are so improbable as to be inconceivable. Everything tends to change to a state of maximum disorder, which is maximum probability, the approach to a completely random state. 'Man', say Angrist and Hepler 'creates local and temporary islands of decreasing entropy in a world in which entropy as a whole certainly increases' (p. 141). A glance round my study certainly confirms that.

On this analogy they describe life as 'the temporary reversal of a universal trend towards maximum disorder' (p. 180). It is 'matter capable of forming itself into a self-reproducing structure that can extract energy from the environment for its first self-assembly'. In other words, it is a thing which defies the Second Law of Thermodynamics. Therefore, it is certainly not a 'thing' as the word is used in physics.

On the other hand, science cannot admit that life is a 'thing' in some sense unknown to physics. The rules of the scientific game exclude metaphysical entities such as the breath that

1. C. P. Snow, *The Two Cultures and the Scientific Revolution*, Cambridge U.P., 1959.
2. Stanley W. Angrist and Loren G. Hepler, *Order and Chaos: Laws of Energy and Entropy*, Penguin, 1973, p. 130.

Jehovah breathed into Adam, or the *élan vital* of the vitalists, which is akin to the old fallacy of explaining fire by a fluid called phlogiston or radio waves by an intangible, imperceptible and unmeasurable fluid called the ether. These tricks do not 'explain', they merely shuffle words around.

And yet in a more respectable sense 'words are things': they exist within a linguistic structure and a context of usage. Men, as the late J. L. Austin put it, can 'do things with words'. That seems so clear as to be banal, and it does not matter in this context whether or not one holds that the use of the concept 'word' requires us to postulate even more abstract concepts – such as concept, idea or meaning.

Certainly it is not the word or concept 'life' which creates life; indeed it is itself an aspect of life and parasitical upon it. But does there 'exist' another horse out of the same stable, called 'information'? Information is that which reduces uncertainty. A switch with two positions must be either ON or OFF – which is it? Knowledge of that is one 'bit' of information, in the ordinary sense of the word 'information'. Legitimately or not, scientific information theory eliminates the knower, and applies the concept of 'BIT' of 'information' to the position of the switch. Perhaps somewhere in this there is a semantic trick – if so, it is a very powerful trick, in that the mathematics and engineering of computers are based on it and so is the construction of steering devices of all kinds. Hence the word 'cybernetics', a convenient label for the new industrial revolution of our time, and also, as Norbert Wiener put it, for *The Human Use of Human Beings*.[1]

It is consistent with the structure of information theory that life should be defined in terms of information, since information is what reduces disorder or randomness – 'life, the temporary reversal of a universal trend towards maximum disorder'. A key to the transmission of information within the world of life has been found in the genetic 'code' of the great molecules of D.N.A. and R.N.A., and the effect of this discovery, with all its ramifications, is to unify the science of life on earth in a most startling way. 'In this elemental drama all life

1. *Cybernetics and Society*, Houghton Mifflin, New York, 1950.

is revealed as one. The events of the process of cell division are common to all earthly life; neither man nor amoeba, the giant sequoia nor the simple yeast cell can long exist without carrying on this process of cell division.'[1]

It is therefore possible to give scientific sense to the statement that life began with certain big molecules of specifiable chemical composition. But to say that does not explain how it happened; still less does it offer what I called a 'cook-book' definition of how to do it. 'They' are working on it, and we are told that there are possible directions of laboratory research; the problem is not in principle insoluble, as is perhaps the problem of the origin of all things. But the genesis of life, if it happened within nature, was a chemical event of absolutely overwhelming improbability. The universe is in some sense or other infinite and in an infinite system all improbabilities actually happen. That is no more paradoxical than it would be to postulate Jehovah the biochemist who suspended the Second Law of Thermodynamics at one infinitely small spot of time – and then retired.

This account has been based only on one popular book, that of Angrist and Hepler: but its exposition reflects the work of greater men – greater, but not necessarily more lucid.

Sohrödinger, who is in some ways my favourite scientific authority, writes in terms of negative entropy: 'Entropy taken with the negative sign is itself a measure of order. Thus the device by which an organism maintains itself stationary at a fairly high level of orderliness ... really consists in continually sucking orderliness from the environment.'[2] I am not sure that it is any easier if one puts it, as do Cannon, Von Bertalanffy and other physiologists and biologists, in terms of homeostasis (equilibrium within an environment), or of exchange across a boundary, or of an adaptive system surviving in an environment. Perhaps all one gets out of these statements positively is that life

1. Rachel Carson, *Silent Spring*, Penguin, 1965, p. 187. Compare Teilhard de Chardin's metaphor, 'From the beginning stages of evolution, the living matter which covers the earth manifests the contours of a single gigantic organism.' *The Phenomenon of Man*, Fontana, 1965.
2. E. Schrödinger (1944), pp. 69, 75.

is not a thing but a set of relationships. Its elements are characterized by interdependence and interaction, and one must think in these terms (as indeed do physicists, chemists and engineers), not in terms of direct lines of cause and effect. Jacques Monod in his rhetorical way[1] invents a word 'teleonomy', direction by a future, by a *projet*, a word which he picks because it can be used to cover both the molecular blueprint in the double helix and also the special characteristic of man in the existential philosophy of Sartre and others.

Monod is as deeply committed as any man to modern scientific materialism, yet there does not seem to be much to choose between his definition and that of Coleridge, quoted by Sherrington, a scientist who was himself a poet: 'I define life as a principle of individuation, or the power that unites a given all into a whole which is presupposed by all its parts.'[2]

These last paragraphs are rather tightly packed and I am not qualified to unpack them because I am only a tertiary source, third man away from truth, in Plato's phrase. But I can say two things with some confidence. Firstly, that these great men have not in fact bridged the gap between the macro-molecule of the gene and the simplest form of living system, whether that is bacillus or virus. The double helix is necessary but not sufficient. Secondly, that in this search for simple forms they have used and emphasized terms which are relevant to the analysis of more complex forms. That analysis can range without breach of continuity over the whole range of living things and their interactions, from the level of the cell to that of the totality of life on earth, including political life.

I have in fact been slipping into this text undefined terms such as negative entropy, orderliness, environment, homeostasis, equilibrium, system, adaptivity, survival, exchange, boundary. The point is that these terms (and some others which are primarily electronic in reference) can be spelt out so as to constitute a theory of political stability and political adaptivity,

1. This is a reference to Mary Warnock's review of Monod's book, *The Listener*, 9 December 1971, p. 788.
2. Sir Charles Sherrington, *Man on His Nature*, Cambridge U.P., 1940, p. 143.

a modern version of the old Positivist or Comtean theme of Order and Progress. Probably the best sources to discuss would be Karl Deutsch for national systems,[1] John Burton for the international system;[2] if I were discussing them professionally I should have to try to specify these terms more exactly, and to puzzle out whether what these authors say is referable to politics scientifically, or only metaphorically, as a sort of poetry. At the end of the day, my conclusion would be, I think, that it is metaphor, but a very powerful metaphor – and part of its strength is that one can use this terminology to organize effectively what information we have about the natural history of life and earth up to and beyond the present age.

Of course these words constitute also the theme of all that has been said and written in the last ten years about ecology and environment, and they are closely allied to the themes of information, automation, and the building of cybernetic machines.

But at this point I want to deal only with Monod's theme of Chance and Necessity. Can the history of life on earth, since its problematic inception, be handled satisfactorily in terms merely of genetic inheritance, chance mutations, natural selection?

Let me now state the case as strongly as I can, leaving objections to the next chapter.

Of course the time scale is unimaginable. I was tempted to reproduce diagrammatic illustrations from Professor Calvin's book on *Chemical Evolution*. But the weakness of such diagrams is that the scale has to be treacherously distorted if it is to find any space at all for mankind, the pinnacle of creation, the tellers of the tale. On the other hand, numbers do not convey a vivid impression. Apparently the first traces of life on earth go back 2000 million years or more; the present species of man, man with the big brain, is no more than 100,000 years old, and perhaps kindred species of man and hominids take the record back to over 10 million years ago, when some species diverged from the forest apes and became creatures of open plains, river banks and sea-shore; competitors with baboons not

1. *The Nerves of Government: Models of Political Communication and Control*, Free Press, New York, 1963.

2. For instance, *World Society*, Cambridge U.P., 1972.

with chimpanzees. A hundred thousand years is a long time in human history, a mere instant in geological time, and it is really more effective to use metaphors rather than figures – man as a swallow flashing through a lighted room, man as creature of a day – the language of Christian hymns, or of the mockery of man by *The Birds* in Aristophanes' comedy.[1]

It may indeed seem odd, scientifically, that there should have been such great biological changes in so short a span as that from ape to man, 20 million years. But it has been a period of rough weather and abrupt climatic changes. One can take up Robert Ardrey's theme of 'man the bad-weather animal',[2] and generalize it as a doctrine of 'man the general purpose animal', one who had avoided the dead end of physical specialization and could find a niche in any ecology. One might add that man has the nasty characteristic, not known to other animals, of eliminating competitors by direct assault and murder,[3] not simply by squeezing them out of a preferred environment. Particularly ruthless selection might well act fast enough to create within the last 100,000 years the animal with the big brain, *homo sapiens*; to quote the archaeologist, Stuart Piggott, man 'as handsome and as wise as us'.[4] It is possible, as has been suggested by some, that this period of rapid physical adaptation is now virtually at an end, its part was played out, once the transition had been made from physical to social evolution.

In the history of that transition, there are certain gaps entailed by the nature of the record. One of them is that between animal and man. We can guess from observation of chimpanzees in the wild that an animal that inherited hands inherited

1. 'Men, creatures of mist, transient as leaves, pithless, moulded of mud, empty and shadowy, wingless, ephemeral, wretched mortals, creatures of dream – give ear to to us, The Birds, immortal, sky-borne, ageless. We think upon what is unchanging, and we shall tell you truth about things above, the nature of birds, the genesis of gods and rivers and Erebus and Chaos.' Aristophanes, *The Birds*, II, 685–91 (my own free translation).

2. *African Genesis*, Fontana/Collins, 1961, ch. 9.

3. Man's 'defence lies mainly in attack. He has set himself deliberately to exterminate those lives which invade and incapacitate and destroy his own.' Sherrington, op. cit., p. 276–7.

4. Stuart Piggott, *Ancient Europe, from the Beginnings of Agriculture to Classical Antiquity*, Edinburgh U.P., 1965, p. 27.

also the extension of hands by the use of whatever 'came to hand',[1] and this is confirmed by the very simple weapons found along with the bones of hominids.[2] Indeed, hominids are, on the face of it, less well qualified than baboons to survive in the open without weapons. Baboons are quite effective social cooperators;[3] hominids must have been even better, and that implies some skill in extemporizing plans of attack and defence at a level above the mentality of lions, wolves, baboons, hyenas, hunting dogs. And that in turn leaves scope for the development of language. Language of course leaves no physical trace, and we have no direct means of telling whether hominids talked. The gap between language and no language is very wide, and has at times seemed comparable to the gap between life and no life. But in this case also the gap is being closed from both sides. There now exist sophisticated studies of how human beings communicate without words – we knew that all along but never noticed it. On the other side there is intensive work on animal communication, including at least a hint that chimpanzees, though they cannot be taught to speak, can be taught to communicate symbolically.[4]

It is particularly difficult to study the dawn of language, but we might perhaps be able to find out more about the use of fire. I think it is fair to say that no non-human can face and manage fire.[5] Fire, in the hand of man, can frighten any animal that has enough intelligence to know fear, and fire in the hand of man

1. For instance, Jane Lawick-Goodall's anecdote and picture of the chimpanzee which used old paraffin cans to make a thunderous noise and so advance its social status (*In the Shadow of Man*, Collins, 1971, p. 109); and the evidence of tool-using accumulated in Edward O. Wilson, *Sociobiology: the New Synthesis*, Harvard U.P., 1975, p. 172 and elsewhere.

2. See, for instance, the references to 'weapons' in the index of Robert Ardrey, *African Genesis*.

3. See, for instance, Eugene Marais, *My Friends the Baboons* and *The Soul of the Ape*, Penguin, 1973; these books remain classics though scientifically obsolete.

4. Eugene Linden, *Apes, Men and Language*, Penguin, 1976, brings the story almost up to date. But it continues.

5. A chimp can light a cigarette? Yes; but I have not found in the literature any report that wild chimpanzees play with fire. 'Fire' does not appear in the index of Wilson's *Sociobiology* (p. 68, n. l).

can change a whole environment, either intentionally or by accident. The traces of man-made fires lie over the whole pre-human world; Lockley, for instance, has many references to the effects of fire on the ecology of New Zealand.[1]

Speech, tools and fire – in terms of systems theory, this was a rich mixture of energy and information, the gunpowder train for an explosion. Perhaps one need not really be surprised that the period from the Old Stone Age to the H-bomb was in genetic terms so short. Once fire had been mastered, the passage had been made from biological to social evolution.

Of course man was not the first social animal. Anything coherent enough to be called an animal is a society of cells; any animal with bisexual reproduction is of necessity social. The insects, as Bronowski noted,[2] very early reached a point at which social structure served them better than physiological evolution. Like all other creatures, they are subject to chance and necessity, and mutant forms continually arise. But they have, to all appearances, ceased to be socially adaptive. Note the formula for a horror film, of which there have been many: one postulates that insects change not physically but socially, and then they can defeat even man.

But man, as Sophocles said, is a very clever fellow, none cleverer.[3] A hundred thousand years ago he lived, to all appearances, a poor life in the open. But he was 'as handsome and as wise as us'. He could be comfortable, he could make pictures, he could make music, he could make poetry, he could make myths and stories and theories. He could make magic. What he needed was a store of energy, to carry him through the bad seasons, for greater ventures in the spring.

That is the story of the fourth gap and breakthrough, which has been called the Neolithic Revolution.[4] It is not much more

1. R. M. Lockley, *Man Against Nature*, André Deutsch, 1970.

2. 'Bronowski's Last Broadcasts. 9: Of Ants and Men', *The Listener*, 26 June 1975.

3. *Antigone*, l. 332 and the following lines.

4. My main sources have been: Stuart Piggott, op. cit., pp. 2–8; I. E. S. Edwards, C. J. Gadd, N. G. L. Hammond (eds.), *The Cambridge Ancient History*, 3rd ed., vol. 1, part 1; Cambridge U.P., 1970; Colin Renfrew (ed.), *British Prehistory: A New Outline*, Duckworth, 1974.

than 10,000 years since man first domesticated food crops and cattle, and became a farmer rather than a nomad and gatherer. Fascinating work has been done in tracing the wild ancestors of the present European strains of domestic animals and food grains, and there is reasonably good evidence which points to the Fertile Crescent of the Middle East, the foothills which intervene between the flood plains of Mesopotamia and the high mountains to the north of them. But this is only part of a new style in archaeology, concerned not with pots, flint axes and other artefacts, but with ecology and environment. Of course a digger is still happy to find a beautiful object, but most of the time he or she is sifting through the dust of hearths and middens, to find traces of grain and animal food from which to reconstruct a pattern of living, and to date it by radio-carbon counts, pollen identification and tree rings. This recent age of prehistory is full of problems, but these too now seem to be within the range of normal science. We now have the tools with which to piece together the story of how the new breed of men conquered the earth. And perhaps from 5000 years ago, with the slow invention of writing and of storytelling in images, we begin to know something of what we cannot otherwise recover – language, mythology, religion, scientific knowledge.

Already something is known of the decisive moves in the West: the move from the foothills down to the great rivers, which could only be mastered by the organized cooperation of many men; the advance across Europe; the relations between the farmers of the Middle East and the horsemen and cattle-men of the great plains; the eventual descent to the coasts and the conquest of the sea. It took perhaps 5000 years for peasant farming to spread from its zone of origin to the furthest extent of Europe in the North and West. Peasant farmers were in Norway and the Northern islands of Scotland by the third millennium B.C., 5000 years ago. There they were blocked for 4000 years, perhaps by deterioration in weather conditions, and the first moves into America came from the East, not from the West. But it is still a riddle whether men in East Asia and Central America and the Pacific invented farming independently or whether the knowledge of farming spread from the West.

Perhaps the idea spread; if so, it was certainly applied independently to any natural resources which came to hand.

This is a story endlessly exciting in its detail and in its variety; and much of it, as for instance the coming of Maori and white men to New Zealand, is almost within living memory. It is the story of how one biological species became dominant. Recently I have seen a good deal of forestry in Scotland, and the image in my mind is that of the year when the canopy closes, when the young trees come together so as to reduce light reaching the ground or to exclude it altogether, and the forest dominates the balance of species.[1] Some species will vanish, others have reservoirs of new growth outside the forest, and will invade it at once if the trees suffer a catastrophe. Men have not a monopoly, but this is the age of man as previous ages have been the age of fish, of insects, of great land-lizards, of great mammals. Some species perished, some reached a peak and have remained static, but all alike were adapted physically to their environment, and all alike had some social structure. The social structure of insect communities has fascinated man for thousands of years, but it has only recently been realized that physical structure and social structure are not intelligible separately. The physiology of a dead beast can be taken to pieces on the dissecting table, but its life is not lived alone. Hence the new domain of ethology, which I think is better called social biology, and the compelling interest of the combination of social biology with ecology: the study of social life in relation to environment.

Within this tradition, it is now part of science to consider the social biology of man in relation to his environment, and the first lesson is that man has broken through into a new dimension of adaptivity, that of social adaptivity, of finding forms of organization which enable him to survive. There are forms of social organization which fit the Arctic fringes or the desert margins; there are other forms which have tamed great rivers, conquered the oceans, built a world-wide industrial complex.

One of the interesting things in this range of study has been the linking of ideas about minds and about machines. Earlier, I

1. Sir Macfarlane Burnet chose a different but cognate metaphor, *Dominant Mammal*, Heinemann, Melbourne, 1970.

scattered around some of the terminology about life and adaptation, and noted that some of the words implied electronic analogies. Among these are the concepts of energy, of information and of requisite variety. An engine will work comfortably within its limits, but it may be pushed to the verge of these limits and may suffer stress. Stress may kill it, or it may set in motion a series of fluctuations, 'hunting', or there may be found a new way, by changing gear as it were, to accelerate through and beyond the barrier. Human societies have passed through all these experiences of stress – steady state, destruction, fluctuation – and so far there has always been some breakthrough somewhere to a new level of control through the creation of a radically new social structure.

One last word on this theme: what I have set out is, from one point of view, a scientific orthodoxy. Each step is, in principle, guaranteed by rigorous argument and observation, and there are characteristically sharp debates between orthodox and heterodox science.[1]

But in this case science doubles as mythology. The steps in the argument are not as difficult to follow as those in physics and cosmology. Nevertheless, even the serious layman has to take much on trust, and for the mass of men the story is a matter of faith, not of science. Most societies (dare I say 'all societies'?) have had a creation myth and a foundation myth: this is how the world was made, this is our place in it.

There are the myths which tell us who we are, which identify us as 'we', sharers in a common destiny. The scientific orthodoxy has not yet wholly displaced older myths of *The Identity of Man*[2] but it is in the ascendant and seems irresistible.

1. The extreme case is that of Immanuel Velikovsky and his theory of catastrophes (A. de Grazia, *The Velikovsky Affair*, Sidgwick & Jackson, 1966). But there is a good deal of acrimony even about the apparently logical problem of 'animal altruism' – surely, a gene for self-sacrificing behaviour would die out? (Richard Dawkins, *The Selfish Gene*, Oxford U.P., 1976).

2. J. Bronowski, Penguin, 1967.

3

The Critics

'Why does philosophy fight over words? The realities of the class struggle are 'represented' by 'ideas' which are 'represented' by words. In scientific and philosophical reasoning, the words (concepts, categories) are 'instruments' of knowledge. But in political, ideological and philosophical struggle, the words are also weapons, explosives or tranquillizers and poisons. Occasionally, the whole class struggle may be summed up in the struggle for one word against another word. Certain words struggle amongst themselves as enemies. Other words are the site of an *ambiguity*: the stake in a decisive but undecided battle.' Interview with Louis Althusser: 'Philosophy as a Revolutionary Weapon', *New Left Review* 64, Nov./ Dec. 1970, p. 10

THUS far, in all innocence, I have set out the perspective of natural history, the context within which one must explore the social biology of man. Once upon a time, this was a theological heresy; now it is the orthodoxy of the scientific world, and it is also a fashion among simple-lifers and new-lifers of various sects. It is true that all orthodoxies should in principle be treated with suspicion. It is also true that there are at least four paradoxes or gaps: the paradox of creation; that of the transition from matter to life; that of the transition from animal to man, from physical to social adaptivity; and finally there is the transition from man as dependent on nature to man the master of nature, the over-arching canopy, the dominant species. Sciences in coalition have focused on these gaps; the coalitions include not only the physical and biological sciences, but also linguistics and archaeology, essentially human sciences, sciences of man in society. Surely this movement must affect, must even include, the other social sciences? I specify, in particular, economic and social history, economics, politics and sociology, because all four of these have been challenged in the last generation by the model of positive science.

Or so I thought until I began to explore this theme in seminars with philosophers and with other social scientists. It seemed to me that this story, these concepts, were beyond controversy, that they were an agreed starting-point or platform, and that the puzzles arose in the attempt to apply them. Not so; here are some radical objections to the whole enterprise, which I must next consider.

I distinguish five of these, as follows: the bad political repute of Social Darwinism; the supposed death of God; the naturalistic fallacy and the attack on 'reductionism' (these three I group together in what follows); the character of human knowledge (phenomenalism since Kant); the character of the human will. If the story I have told is indeed good science, it must be prepared to admit amendment, both to incorporate new findings and to re-state its principles in such a way as to meet logical objections. I must confess that I did not realize at first how strong these objections were and how strongly felt, and that they must be met before one can proceed from the orthodoxy of the biological text-books to its political and social application. The more I read the more clearly I see that the biologists have blundered unwittingly into a spider's web of philosophical distinctions, rivalries and commitments. This is dull stuff compared with the excitement of scientific discovery, but it has had a central place in the European tradition of philosophical inquiry. 'Words are also weapons.'

The first objection, then, is that we have been here before, and that 'biologism' failed us then. Once the battle against the old theological orthodoxy had been won (and victory at the centre was gained in the 1870s – though pockets of resistance remained in the American Bible Belt even in the 1920s[1]), the emphasis switched from science to ideology. The phrase 'survival of the fittest' is obscure, even tautologous: the evidence of fitness lies in the fact of survival, the prolific and adaptable weak may displace those who appear strong. But it was equally easy to interpret survival to mean victory in battle, 'Nature, red

1. The famous landmark is that of the Scopes trial in Dayton, Tennessee, in July 1925, involving a statute which banned the teaching of evolution in public schools.

in tooth and claw,'[1] a Hobbesian war of all against all. This was not what Darwin, or even Huxley, meant, but they could be taken in that sense, before the re-discovery of Mendel in about 1900, the rise of mathematical genetics and molecular biology and (particularly since 1945) the patient work done in ethology and ecology. Evolutionary theory was called in to support a much older ideology, that life is war, and the strongest are the best. That doctrine was generally thought to be nasty, as expressed in Plato's parody of Thrasymachus, in Machiavelli, Hobbes, de Sade,[2] Gobineau. But some nice people took it up at the end of the nineteenth century, in the name of 'eugenics', the selective breeding of better human beings – and the discouragement of breeding from 'bad stock'. And others, not so nice, hitched evolutionary ideology to the creed of nationality and race. The words 'Social Darwinism' (invented by later scholars, I think)[3] came to stand for a mood rather than a movement: a number of confused and optimistic coteries swept aside by the torrent of events in central Europe before and after the First World War, and culminating in the ideology of *Mein Kampf*, the mobilization of racism as the word of power with which to defeat Marxist revolution. The intellectual horror of the story matches its physical horror: science, optimism, benevolence, patriotism degenerating into slime under the pressure of war, disease, poverty, idleness.

Therefore, it is assumed that to say Social Darwinism is to say 'racism', that to talk of the natural history of man is to use dirty words. Hence the unpleasant attacks on psychologists such as Eysenck and Jensen who make the attempt to relate genetic inheritance to varieties of psychological talent and capacity. Those who attack them scarcely seem to realize that it is they, the attackers, who now represent orthodoxy persecuting deviants, lonely inquirers. Orthodoxy has totally discarded Social

1. Tennyson, *In Memoriam*, lvi.
2. Marquis de Sade (Noelle Chatelet, ed.), *Système d'Aggression: Textes politiques et philosophiques*, Aubier-Montaigne, Paris, 1972.
3. R. J. Halliday, 'Social Darwinism: a Definition', *Victorian Studies* 14, 1971, pp. 389–405); 'The Sociological Movement, the Sociological Society, and the Genesis of Academic Sociology in Britain', *Sociological Review* 16, new series, 1968, pp. 377–98.

Darwinism, in the sense that virtually no one sees genetic selection as a major continuing factor in human history now. Of course genetic differences exist: we have only to look at ourselves and our kindred to see that. But the key to man's biological success in the last 100,000 years is to be found not in the breeding of supermen but in the very much faster and more fertile history of social adaptation. The human gene pool is very rich: within it no two of us are the same (except perhaps identical twins), and yet within a normal range of variation all men are genetically equal. This is now a scientific orthodoxy, and it is good science to seek to qualify it and make it more precise. But there is no scientific basis whatever for the resurrection of the kind of Social Darwinism to which racialists once looked for support.[1]

I have heard a distinguished political scientist blast off in the same persecuting tone of voice against Konrad Lorenz and the attempt to interpret human society in terms of the social biology of animals. That interpretation was fashionable in the 1960s, and it is easy to see why that should be so. On the one hand, men feel deep kinship and sentimental curiosity in relation to animals; animal fables, animal magic, can be traced back as far as it is possible to trace mythology at all, and even in our urban society there is a certain home-sickness, and a ready market, for good stories and pictures about animals. Indeed, the market for pets and pet foods flourishes in a rather embarrassing way; you will not be welcome in England if you explain (as *New Society* did) how much dogs eat, what infections they spread, how they foul public parks.[2] On the other hand, the period was one of human anxiety about human violence; one line of thought was to blame it on our animal inheritance (which of course exists) rather than on our specifically human social structures and social stress. Add to this Lorenz's special

1. It is fair to note that Professor C. D. Darlington holds a relatively strong view of the association between caste, class and breeding: *The Evolution of Man and Society*, Allen & Unwin, 1969, and 'Race, Class and Culture' in J. W. S. Pringle (ed.), *Biology and the Human Sciences*, Clarendon Press, 1972.

2. Tom Forester, 'Animal Planning', *New Society*, 8 May 1975, p. 325.

nostalgic charm, and we had a short period of mythology in which it was the fashion (as it had been often before) to think of men in terms of aggression and territory, of wolves and dogs and geese and jackdaws.

In denouncing all this my colleague was scientifically right. But he allowed his aggression to rub off on the whole science of social biology, and that was quite wrong. Lorenz had been only one among a notable group of creative scientists in that field, and practically no other serious scientist has gone along with him in converting science into parable. I rely here very largely on my old Oxford and Glasgow colleague, Tony Barnett, now professor at the Australian National University:[1] but what little I have read confirms my impression that the present generation of ethologists,[2] and of ecologists too, is acutely aware of the danger to science that lurks in the language of metaphor. I referred in Chapter 2 to the explosive character of human mastery of language, tools and fire; the consequences of these are intelligible scientifically but not in terms of animal mythology. The true myth, the veridical fable, is that of Prometheus, Bound and Unbound, the bringer of fire, the defender of free human intelligence, the rebel against the old gods.

There are other objections to the approach through natural history that disturb me radically. That one does not.

Nor am I at all disturbed by religious scruples. It is true that God is dead, as Nietzsche put it, but what has been lost is merely the trick of using 'God' to fill gaps in science. In the scheme of natural history there remains the eternal problem of the uncaused cause – what was there when there was nothing? The first chapter of Genesis seems to me to have one good answer, a poetic or mythological answer; or one can let the fly out of the bottle in a linguistic way; or one can adopt Edmund Burke's attitude that 'we should reverence what we cannot presently comprehend'. But at other stages of scientific investigation scientists do not need the hypothesis of God any more

1. For instance, ' "*Instinct*" *and* "*Intelligence*": *the Science of Behaviour in Animals and Man*', Macgibbon & Kee, 1967.

2. For instance, R. A. Hinde, *Biological Bases of Human Social Behaviour*, McGraw-Hill, 1974.

than they need hypotheses about little green men from Venus in their flying saucers. As the social anthropologist Evans-Pritchard put it, 'science deals with relations, not with origins and essences'.[1]

It is unfashionable and perhaps injudicious for a social scientist even to mention the word God with a capital G. But I cannot help feeling that the answer lies somewhere in the zone of the late Professor Evans-Pritchard's reverent approach to African religion.[2] The tribal African was a wonderful field naturalist, and as good a practising technologist as any man. What puzzled him was not that one kind of plant is poisonous, one kind of tree is good for making bows, or that animal predators and prey move in regular and intelligible patterns. The puzzle is that of the individual case: why did that accident, that illness, fall on me, my son, my wife, and not on one of hundreds of thousands of others who were at risk at that time? Why me? Science can go only a little way to answer that sort of question, and in any case a scientific explanation is not the sort of answer one wants. For explanation, and the comfort of explanation, one must look to a different quarter. There is plenty of evidence that that search for comfort goes on as actively as it ever did. One must put oneself in the hands of the Lord. What else is there to do?

Certainly I see no conflict whatever between religion in that sense and the natural history of man.

The third line of objection is more complex. I met it first in the accusation that I was committing the 'naturalistic fallacy', a crime excoriated by G. E. Moore (the most influential English philosopher of his generation) in his first book, *Principia Ethica,* published in 1903.

The book is famous among other things for its contemptuous dismissal of Herbert Spencer – 'So much for Mr Spencer' (p. 54) – who had been for fifty years the spokesman of social evolution and died that year at the age of eighty-three. G. E. Moore was then thirty, and belonged to that brash and brilliant Cam-

1. *Theories of Primitive Religion*, Oxford U.P., 1965, p. 111.
2. Op. cit., in the last chapter of that book.

bridge period from which came the work of Whitehead and Russell on *Principia Mathematica* (1919), of I. A. Richards on *The Principles of Literary Criticism* (1924) and the life work of J. M. Keynes, culminating in *The General Theory of Employment, Interest and Money* (1936). It was also one of the great periods of discovery in physics at the Cavendish Laboratory.

I don't much like G. E. Moore's manners in that book nor his style of argument; it is so easy for a young man to find obscurities and inconsistencies in the work of an author who has been writing for fifty years, and it does not advance philosophy.[1] But with the weight of Cambridge behind it, his attack on Spencer killed 'evolutionary ethics' stone dead. Moore's own argument is not entirely clear to me, but its main point is that goodness (specifically, moral goodness, I think) is something qualitatively unique, analogous to a colour (insofar as it admits any analogies at all), and that you can no more define goodness in terms of its origins or its purposes than you can define the colour yellow in terms of physical components. It is simply not that kind of thing at all.

Hume does not appear in Moore's index, but to me this seems to be an incident in the long debate about deducing values from facts, begun by a paragraph in David Hume's *Treatise* (1739) about the logical impossibility of passing from 'is' to 'ought' whether deductively or by induction. The best answer I have found, in a long but very superficial acquaintance with the vast literature, is that our selection of what to call a fact is settled for us by social values and indeed by social conflict, and that value – the word 'ought' – is senseless without a context. But the logic of the fact/value dichotomy is definitionally immaculate, and one has to step carefully.

1. But I would not go so far as A. M. Quinton, *The Nature of Things*, Routledge & Kegan Paul, 1973: 'The origin of this ethical pre-occupation is Moore's purported demonstration that naturalism is a fallacy (*Principia Ethica*, ch. 1). The extraordinary thinness of Moore's arguments poses something of a problem, for seldom can such an uncomplex array of sophisms have exercised such intellectual authority.' Moore grew wiser and more amiable.

One must be wary also of two other philosophical booby-traps: the question of mind/body dualism, and the slander of 'reductionism'.

The former raises the question of 'common sense' – a view of the world defended by Moore in his later years. Common sense says that one experiences two worlds: to take extreme examples, on the one hand we experience pain and no one else experiences 'my pain';[1] on the other hand, we test the firmness of a piece of ground and if it bears my weight it will bear your weight (you are smaller than I am). The extreme examples provoke one to imagine paradoxes: on the one hand, the possibility of feeling another's pain, extra-sensorily – the pain of a beloved friend, Christ's pain on the Cross; on the other hand, the possibility that the ground felt as solid is 'really' a carefully prepared trap, such as men set for animals.

There are also marginal cases in the proposed dualism of mind and body, internal and external senses; colour and sound are rather more ambiguous than pain. In a sense no two persons (not defective in sight or hearing) see the same picture, hear the same symphony, because their vision and their hearing differ slightly in natural endowment, differ much more in training and social environment. Hence the distinction (which is as old as Lucretius) between primary and secondary qualities. Colour can be 'reduced' to wave-lengths, and these are 'real', in that they are inter-personal. They can be measured, and measurements can be compared. Primary qualities are in 'nature', secondary qualities are 'in the mind'.

> You should not suppose the whiteness you see in an object
> Means whiteness in its elements (i.e., its 'atoms'), or that black objects
> Come from elements which themselves are black;
> Nor indeed, whatever colour an object has
> That it is made of elements of that colour.

1. There is a psychological word, 'affect', sometimes used vaguely, which might usefully be specialized in this sense; cf. Paul D. MacLean, 'The Paranoid Streak in Man', in Arthur Koestler and J. R. Smythies, *Beyond Reductionism: New Perspectives in the Life Sciences.* Proceedings of the Alpbach Symposium 1968, Hutchinson, 1969.

The elements of matter have no colour at all,
Neither like the objects they form nor yet unlike them.[1]

This certainly seems to be an odd business, and it has generated much mythology, in all ages and conditions of life. The soul has vanished from philosophy, I think, but ghosts and extra-sensory perception still haunt us. Above all we have 'mind', the ghost in the machine, as Gilbert Ryle called it in *The Concept of Mind*.[2]

Personally, I find myself in sympathy with the 'common sense' philosophers, the later Moore, Ryle, Quinton, Smart.[3] People are pretty well agreed on the way things are in general, and also about our ignorance of them in particular. Do not let us entangle ourselves in words which positively impede our life-long search for understanding. And we can do that without committing the sin of reductionism.[4]

The sin has various spheres of action: to reduce mind to body – to the atoms and the void; to reduce biology to physics and chemistry, to reduce man to animal. The great reductionist of our time is the French micro-biologist, Jacques Monod, who has made direct appeal to the tradition of Lucretius in his public lectures on 'Chance and Necessity', which managed to provoke Marxists and idealists to equal expressions of indignation – he chose his enemies deliberately and struck a dramatic pose as champion of the universal principles of scientific inquiry against all comers.

Surely this also is a question to be handled piece-meal? In

1. Lucretius II, 731–8, translated by C. H. Sisson, p. 63. Compare Democritus, Fragment 9: 'Sweet and bitter are subjective, so are hot and cold, so are colours; the only objective reality is that of the atoms and the void.' Diels-Kraug, *Fragmente der Vorsokratiker*, Weidmann, Berlin-Grünewald, 1952.

2. Hutchinson, 1949.

3. *Philosophy and Scientific Realism*, Routledge & Kegan Paul, 1963; *Between Science and Philosophy*, Random House, 1968.

4. Some relevant books: C. H. Waddington, *The Ethical Animal*, Allen & Unwin, 1960; Arthur Koestler and J. R. Smythies (eds.), op. cit.; Marjorie Grene (ed.), *Interpretations of Life and Mind: Essays around the Problem of Reduction*, Routledge & Kegan Paul, 1971; R. J. Spilsbury, *Providence Lost*, Oxford U.P., 1974.

one sense, chemistry has been reduced to physics, and there is continuity of theory from atomic nucleus to very large molecules. But some of these large molecules are the product of life, and transmit 'information' from one generation to the next. Others are mind-bending drugs; it is said to be easy to synthesize L.S.D., but there is nothing in physics or chemistry which could 'explain' its effect on the inner vision. We can't, in that sense, 'explain' even the beneficent and deadly properties of alcohol.

In the present context, the battle against reductionism is being fought mainly on the frontier between life and non-life, and various heroic figures can be discerned battling in the mist: Michael Polanyi, Ludwig von Bertalanffy, Paul Weiss, Jean Piaget, W. H. Thorpe, mustered under the management of such entrepreneurs as Marjorie Grene and Arthur Koestler. But it is not easy to see a pattern, still harder to see why controversy need be bitter. On the one hand, living matter has very odd properties which contradict the laws of physics and chemistry. On the other hand, vitalism is dead; life is matter, not matter *plus* an ill-defined and superfluous ghost. One attractive line of answer is that life is a form of order, that order (as distinct from chaos, 'the heat death' foretold by the Second Law) is equivalent to information, and that life (all life on earth) arises from a code of information implanted in the big molecules of D.N.A. and transmitted by them.

This is attractive, because it promises continuity without reduction. There is no breach in the unity of science, but to seek for unity between life and the physical sciences modifies the physical sciences by the introduction of a new (and difficult) concept. Old biology (it is said) cannot plausibly be reduced to old physics and chemistry, but we can understand both more deeply and reshape them.

And so too for the supposed reduction of man to animal; test it, argue about it, and you will gain a better understanding of the links and also of the distinctions. The chain of science is in principle unbroken – but for humans humans are special. All right, for worms worms are special; for wolves wolves are

44

special. But we are, as a matter of fact, human here and now, whatever our origin. We are special.

I do not think, re-reading chapter two, that I have committed the sins of naturalism or reductionism – as yet. But it is my intention in later chapters to look at the problems and theories and institutions of human adaptivity today. The reader is fore-warned.

The second battery of criticism is based on a complex series of arguments which may be called, perhaps pedantically, phenomenological. To simplify rashly, they all stem from the confrontation of Kant and Hume in the latter part of the eighteenth century: a European system-builder, specifically a German *Gelehrter*, whatever the truth about his claim to a Scottish grandfather, facing the ironic lucidity of David Hume, a man of the enlightenment who was as much at home in Paris as in Edinburgh. Hume's paradox was that men perceive not 'things' but 'appearances', and that their knowledge of things is no more than probable inference. It seems at first sight a simple acceptance of the facts of 'science' that what we receive through the senses are not things but 'sense-data'; messages perhaps, but we can never compare the message received with the message sent. Such is our human predicament. Hume was by no means a universal sceptic and destroyer; temperamentally, he could get along in life very well with reasonable probabilities, and that was the stance which he recommended to mankind as the best formula for a kind and comfortable existence in a precarious world.

But for academic philosophers this was a philosophic scandal, and 'to refute Hume' became a necessary pastime for 'believers' of all sects, conservative and radical alike. Some moderns (I really know only the work of J. L. Austin) have tried to 'let the fly out of the bottle' by attacking the language of sense-data as alien to ordinary speech and conceptually inappropriate – a Humeàn move to outflank Hume. Kant, taking a position fun-damentally more radical, accepted Hume, and indeed went beyond him to assert that out of sense-data men build a world, and that there exist, built into rational men, certain rules for construction (and for action also) which embody reason itself. Man cannot venture beyond the bounds of reason so as to know 'the thing in itself', but reason and its intuitions are the highest things in man's small universe. Hence, one of Kant's few ventures into eloquence: 'there are two things that fill my mind anew with wonder and awe, the more often, the more deeply I dwell on them; the sky and its stars above me, the moral law within'.[1]

Kant wrote so much, in such terrifyingly abstract German prose, that one needs to remind oneself continually that he had a mind of exceptional openness, honesty and range, and that in some queer sense he, the wizened little man in a provincial German town, was a citizen of the world in his time, a Wordsworthian, a romantic.

In the last few years, radical thought in the West has been working backward into its past because present questions compel it to do so; from the Marxists to Marx, from Marx to Hegel, from Hegel to Kant. It is perhaps a quixotic and self-defeating exercise; but it makes sense to me now (as it did not at the time) that I was required to read the *Critique*, under Harry Weldon's guidance,[2] some forty-five years ago.

The reason is that one can see Kant as the source from which three tendencies diverge – phenomenological, idealist, Marxist; and each of them has many by-ways. But they would converge to attack my innocent exposition of the natural history of man.

To imagine (what is impossible) a single objector, his comment might be phrased like this: 'This long story of the Ascent of Man is your own construct. On that base you cannot build.' To put it in other words: but for man, this story of man as a part of nature could not exist. Nature is dependent on man just as a dream depends on a dreamer. Man is bound within the circle of his collective dream. This is of course the argument in chapter four of Lewis Carroll's *Alice through the Looking-Glass* – 'Why, you're only a sort of thing in the Red King's dream,' says Tweedledee, and, adds Tweedledum, 'If that there King was to wake, you'd go out – bang! – just like a candle.'

1. *The Critique of Practical Reason*, Conclusion.
2. T. D. Weldon, *Kant's Critique of Pure Reason*, Clarendon Press, 1955.

They cheerfully agree that they are characters in the same dream, and all Alice can say in the end is 'I know they're talking nonsense, and it's foolish to cry about it.'

Once upon a time God had to do duty as Red King, as eternally present observer and guarantor of reality. Most people know the Oxford limericks on this theme, the first of them attributed to Monsignor Ronny Knox:[1]

> There once was a man who said 'God
> Must think it exceedingly odd
> If he finds that this tree
> Continues to be
> When there's no one about in the Quad'.

To which God answers, in a somewhat off-hand Oxford manner:

> Dear Sir, Your astonishment's odd:
> *I* am always about in the Quad.
> And that's why the tree
> Will continue to be,
> Since observed by Yours faithfully, God.

There is a Max Beerbohm cartoon in which an elderly Matthew Arnold is confronted by his small niece, Mary Augusta, later known as Mrs Humphry Ward, a most improving late Victorian novelist: 'Why, dear Uncle Matthew,' she says, 'cannot you be always wholly serious?' There has always been a strand in English philosophy which cannot quite keep a straight face in discussing the metaphysical agonies of European (particularly German) philosophers and their young students. It harks back to Dr Samuel Johnson and his refutation of Bishop Berkeley's elegant and paradoxical idealism: Johnson struck his foot 'with mighty force against a large stone, till he rebounded from it, saying, "I refute it *thus*." '[2] If you take phenomenalism too seriously it leaves you with nothing, not even with solipsism, because a man cannot talk even to himself unless he gets the language of talk somehow from the experience of talking to

1. Used similarly in Colin Blakeman's Reith Lectures, *The Listener*, 25 November 1976, p. 667.
2. Boswell, *Life of Johnson*, 6 Aug. 1763.

another. It is not profound but merely silly to dismiss all constructs alike as collectively subjective, mere projections of shared states of consciousness, men as creatures existing only in one another's dreams. The hard and interesting soluble problems (this ironical philosophy would say) begin when one has to try to distinguish between different kinds of construct: between mythology and science, or (at the level of action) between technology, ritual, and magic.

Judged by criteria relevant to that debate it seems to me that the evolutionary story of man is now quite a good piece of science. It has an overall shape or *Gestalt* of a persuasive kind, and that conceptual framework is the ground of a large number of factual propositions, many of which can be tested in various ways, even though they are propositions about individual events in the past.[1] Such propositions are known to be slippery in a scientific sense, and perhaps one should make no more claim than is implied by Popper's word 'conjectures'.[2] But these are conjectures, not dreams. It is in a sense true that each of us draws individuality from the reflection we see in the eyes of others: but the web of images is not dream but social reality.

Nevertheless, I gladly agree that the distinction between science and subjectivity is not clear-cut. It is not accidental that this kind of science is being done at this juncture of man's history. It is indeed a construct of man in the late twentieth century, an ideology in which we face a complex set of problems which are both technological and mythological. Who are we? and what are we to do next?

That will serve as a link to the third objection, or family of objections. In what sense, if any, is there a self-conscious entity or community called Man, which has the capacity to spread out a fan of possible futures, like a fan of cards, to deliberate, to choose and to act? After all, the schema of evolutionary adap-

1. Postulate the disappearance of all men today. Are we to believe that evolution would repeat itself, and in due course produce men once more? Of course not: the specific conjuncture cannot recur, even in an infinity of time and space.

2. Karl Popper, *Conjectures and Refutations; The Growth of Scientific Knowledge*, Routledge & Kegan Paul, 1963.

tation says No to all these questions. Adaptation is not chosen nor willed; it happens, by chance and necessity, whereas man, say countless objectors, possesses will guided by self-consciousness.

This comes up from all quarters in the audience, quite without regard to left or right in the political spectrum, and it is rather arbitrary that I choose to take it up here within the context of modern Marxism and Maoism. The point could equally well be made from some points of view within Christian theology, from some points of view which seek to avoid doctrinal commitment. I take up the Marxist aspect largely because one cannot now teach politics in any Western university without facing the complexities of neo-Marxism. These are often tedious and perverse, but they 'weigh like an incubus' upon the mind of the present generation of students.[1] It is quite pointless to shut one's eyes and hope that the problem will go away; it will not.

The dominant passage is well-known but it seems worthwhile to quote a little more than the usual text, because the text has a context and also because it is an example of Marx's writing at its very best, both in style and in the capacity to bear down on a petty historical villain with all the force of great principles and wide perspectives.

Men make their own history, but they do not make it just as they please; they do not make it under circumstances chosen by themselves, but under circumstances directly found, given and transmitted from the past. The tradition of all the dead generations weighs like an incubus on the brain of the living. And just when they seem engaged in revolutionizing themselves and things, in creating something entirely new, precisely in such epochs of revolutionary crisis they anxiously conjure up the spirits of the past to their service and borrow from them names, battle slogans and costumes in order to present the new scene of world history in this time-honoured disguise and this borrowed language. Thus Luther donned the mask of the Apostle Paul, the Revolution of 1789–1814 draped itself alternately as the Roman Republic and the Roman Empire, and the Revolution of 1848 knew of nothing better to do than to parody in turn 1789, and the revolutionary tradition of 1793 to 1795. In like

1. Written after the 1975 examinations; in 1977 they seem better informed – but bored.

manner the beginner, who has learnt a new language, always trans-
lates it back into his mother tongue, but he has assimilated the spirit
of the new language and can produce freely in it only when he
moves in it without calling to mind his ancestral tongue.

But closer consideration of this historical conjuring with the dead
reveals at once a salient difference. Camille Desmoutins, Danton,
Robespierre, Saint-Just, Napoleon, the heroes as well as the parties
and the masses of the old French Revolution, performed the task of
their time in Roman costume and with Roman phrases, the task of
releasing and establishing modern *bourgeois* society. The first mentioned knocked the feudal basis to pieces and cut off the feudal
heads which had grown from it. The other created inside France the
conditions under which free competition could first be developed,
the parcelled landed property exploited, the unfettered productive
power of the nation employed, and outside the French borders he
everywhere swept the feudal form away, so far as it was necessary
to furnish bourgeois society in France with a suitable up-to-date
environment on the European Continent. The new social formation
once established, the antediluvian Colossuses disappeared and with
them the resurrected Romans – the Brutuses, Gracchi, Publicolas,
the Tribunes, the Senators and Caesar himself. Bourgeois society in
its sober reality has begotten its true interpreters and mouth-
pieces . . .[1]

And it is indeed difficult to stop the quotation there, because
what Marx has written up to this point leads to what follows
and gains force and point from it. As someone said of Burke,
Marx 'winds into his subject like a serpent'.[2]

I do not think that the passage as a whole admits ambiguity:
but take the first four lines out of context, then look for parallel
texts (using one's scriptural concordance) in Marx himself, in
Engels, in Lenin. One has then set up a theological situation:

> There's a great text in Galatians,
> Once you trip on it entails
> Twenty-nine distinct damnations,
> One sure, if another fails.[3]

There is a deviation to the Left into adventurism, to the Right

1. *The Eighteenth Brumaire of Louis Bonaparte*, 1852.
2. Oliver Goldsmith, quoted in Boswell, *Life of Johnson*, 10 May 1773.
3. Browning, 'Soliloquy of the Spanish Cloister'.

into economism – but that over-simplifies and I am reminded of the title of a recent seminar paper by David MacLellan – 'Will the real Karl Marx please stand up?'

To put it more ponderously, and also in a way exactly relevant to the present question, I quote two sentences from an Italian Marxist, Sebastiano Timpanaro, translated in the *New Left Review*. 'Perhaps the sole characteristic common to all contemporary varieties of Western Marxism is, with very few exceptions, their concern to defend themselves against the accusation of materialism. Gramscian or Togliattian Marxists, Hegel-Existentialist Marxists, Neo-Positivizing Marxists, Freudian or Structuralist Marxists, despite the profound dissensions which otherwise divide them, are at one in rejecting all suspicion of collusion with 'vulgar' or 'mechanical' materialism; and they do so with such zeal as to cast out, together with mechanism or vulgarity, materialism *tout court*.'[1] In terms of my experience this is correct; the theme of the natural history of mankind now runs into Marxist attack of a kind which is difficult to pin down and answer.

On the one hand, there is no doubt that Marx and Engels believed in Darwinism. There is extant a letter from Marx to Engels in which he enthusiastically welcomed *The Origin of Species*. True, they use untranslatable German adjectives such as *grob* and *plump*[2] to describe English methods, meaning perhaps merely that Darwin had not had a Hegelian education.[3] But the guarantee of Marx's sincerity lies in the elaborately courteous exchange of letters with Darwin about the possibility that Darwin might accept the dedication of *Das Kapital* on its first publication. This reads as if Marx genuinely looked to Darwin as a teacher, in spite of his antipathy to Malthus, whose theme inspired both Darwin and A. R. Wallace.

1. *New Left Review* 85, May–June 1974, p. 3.
2. The definitions in an old edition of Flügel's dictionary are delightful:
Grob: gross, clumsy, homely, crass, uncouth, unpolished, ill-bred, rustic, clownish, boorish, churlish, insolent.
Plump: heavy, bulky, cumbrous, blockish, awkward, unwieldy, blunt, coarse, bluff, clumsy.
3. Valentino Gerratana, *Ricerche di Storia del Marxismo*, Rome, 1972; see also *New Left Review* 82, Nov./Dec. 1973, p. 63.

Indeed, Engels in his old age, when he acted independently of Marx, was strongly attracted by 'the natural history of man', and in consequence has been attacked by some neo-Marxists as a vulgar materialist of the school of Haeckel – whereas others defend him.

The question one wants to pose is: 'What would Marx say about the natural history of man, of chance and necessity, supposing that he were alive now, young and in full vigour, and in possession of the content of natural science as it now stands – with all its gaps and imperfections?' The question is perhaps a silly one and unanswerable; as silly as to ask what Jesus Christ would have said. The faithful Marxist or Christian must either accept authority, or apply his own intelligence, experience and courage to questions not answered by the founder. But there is still no good book (to my knowledge) on Marx, Engels and the moving frontier of science in their time. They certainly read widely in biology and anthropology, but what did they think of the revolutions in medicine, mathematics, physics, chemistry and engineering science which were being made by their contemporaries? My impression is that, in spite of their wide reading, they lagged a little behind the moving front of scientific inquiry. But to attempt an answer would require an immense knowledge of the texts in their context, that of the torrential flow of mid-nineteenth-century science; what 'the fathers' might have read – what they did read.

There is, however, one sidelight which I have not seen noted elsewhere. As I mentioned in Chapter 2, when I was young at Balliol I worked quite hard on the Roman poet, Lucretius – and so did Marx, at much the same age. I had not looked at Lucretius for years until the present theme brought me back to him, and it seemed right to dedicate this little book to him. The science is good, of its time; the poetry is great and for all time. And after 2000 years no man has achieved the same, or even attempted it.[1]

Lucretius had two Greek sources: Democritus of the fifth

1. Desmond King-Héle has recently done a good deal for the poetical reputation of Charles Darwin's grandfather, Erasmus Darwin, a good biologist and a brisk versifier; a very singular person in his own right, but not a Lucretius.

century B.C. and Epicurus who lived at the end of the fourth century. Democritus, the scientist, founded the doctrine of Chance and Necessity, the postulates of scientific method accepted by Jacques Monod. Epicurus the moralist, in the period of great empires and quiet despair, deduced from it a doctrine which we still call 'epicurean'. The gods existed, but dwelt apart, above the terrestrial sphere:

> Live and lie reclined
> On the hills like Gods together, careless of mankind.
> For they lie beside their nectar, and the bolts are hurled
> Far below them in the valleys, and the clouds are lightly curled.
> Round their golden houses, girdled with the gleaming world.[1]

Epicurus deduced value from fact, from science a happy, hippy detachment. Lucretius celebrated them both, fact and value, making a poem out of science moralized.

> A Greek man was the first to raise his eyes,
> Daring to look at God and stand against him.
> He took no notice of all of the thunder and lightning,
> Religious refutations merely incited him;
> He said he would expose the secrets of nature
> And so, by force of intelligence, and no other,
> He pierced beyond the flaming walls of the world,
> Paraded up and down the whole immensity
> And came back a winner with explanations for everything,
> – What could happen, what not, and what were the limits,
> All fixed and measured, of every nature and thing.
> And so he had religion under his feet.
> He won, and as a result we have no superiors.[2]

But it is hard to see Lucretius as 'epicurean'; what he claims for himself from the gods is freedom, not easy living.

Marx's doctoral thesis (he was then about twenty-three, and still a poet) deals with Democritus and Epicurus, and its theme is to distinguish their separate contributions to the Epicurean tradition, which he does in a subtle and convincing way, from fragmentary evidence. Cyril Bailey (a most un-Marxist man) had read the thesis and thought highly of it.[3] But he never saw

1. Tennyson, 'The Lotus-Eaters'.
2. Lucretius I, 66–79, translated by C. H. Sisson, p. 17.
3. 'Karl Marx on Greek Atomism', *Classical Quarterly* 22, 1928, p. 205.

Marx's notebooks,[1] which seem to show that Marx much preferred Lucretius to either Democritus or Epicurus. At the head of that notebook he wrote 'can't use Lucretius much' (p. 144). But he went on to copy out by hand many pages of Lucretius' poem. Either he had been warned off Lucretius by his professor or he realized for himself that Lucretius had put so powerful a stamp of genius in his work that it was impossible to deduce what he had found in his (frankly, rather boring) sources.

At any rate, the notes end with comments by young Marx which I have not seen quoted elsewhere. He hails Lucretius, father of the natural history of man, as 'the fresh keen poetical master of the world' (p. 154):[2] a model for philosophy as Marx defined it – 'the true basis of research in philosophy', says Marx, 'is to have a mind free and sharp' (p. 154). Lucretius, he says, is the truly Roman heroic poet: his heroes are the atoms (and I cannot do justice to the German) 'indestructible, impenetrable, well-armed, lacking all qualities but these; a war of all against all, the stubborn form of eternal substance, Nature without gods, gods without a world' (p. 170). And at the end of the thesis Marx adopts Prometheus as his exemplar and hero.

This is Marx working in a field of pure scholarship and yet emotionally involved. It seems to me that his emotion is one for a natural history of man, a positive science of man, but one illuminated by poetry and by intense ethical concern.

To prove this, or to refute it, would need more learning than I have; but I should like to argue that for Marx a natural history of man was necessary but not sufficient. Darwin's approach was the right one; theology and mysticism must be expelled from the science of man and society. Yet such a science must in its nature speak from a point of view, must seek moral goals, must itself be part of the social system which it analyses. The answer is sometimes said to lie in the dialectic. I find it more convincing to believe that Marx could not formulate the paradox adequately except in the language of myth and symbol.

1. Published in the *Ergänzungsband* of the Marx-Engels complete works, vol. I, Dietz, Berlin, 1968.
2. Perhaps an echo of Goethe's poem on the young Prometheus, which Marx must have known?

4

Limits of Growth

MY starting point in this inquiry can be illustrated by a quotation from the Preface to the second edition of Sir Charles Sherrington's famous book *Man on His Nature*.[1]

'The book [i.e., *Man on His Nature*, 1951 edition] stresses the view that man is a product, like so much else, of the play of natural forces acting on the material and under the conditions past and present obtaining on the surface of our planet.'

Notice that Sherrington does not say that man is *merely* such a product; nor did I. But listeners insert or imply that term, and a bald statement of scientific orthodoxy provokes unexpected opposition. Indeed it involves one in debate about the intellectual history of the last two hundred years, and my effort to summarize that debate, briefly and schematically, will not satisfy philosophers and other specialists. Regard it merely as a set of warning notices, 'This ground is treacherous,' or (to use Michael Oakeshott's guide-book analogy) *nur für die Schwindelfreie*[2] – avoid this path if heights make you feel dizzy.

Two of these notices I am inclined to disregard. The story of 'Social Darwinism', the path from scientism to racism, is surely now so familiar that the broken ground is fenced beyond the risk of accident. And the debate, surely, has clarified the position about personal religion, as distinct from theological dogmatism and orthodoxy. The former is not, and never has been, threatened by the procedures of scientific inquiry.

But the other warnings cannot be treated so lightly. The first of them attacks reductionism; that is to say that it sees the words 'nothing but' inserted in Sherrington's sentence, and if this reduction is accepted it follows that the only ethic available to man is one deduced from 'the play of natural forces'. I am a

1. Cambridge U.P., 1940, 1951.
2. 'Political Education', *Rationalism in Politics and Other Essays*, Methuen, 1962.

little sceptical about Moore's attack on the naturalistic fallacy; but I am now committed to examine the interplay between 'is' and 'ought', and I know that I must walk warily, lest science slide over into ideology.

Secondly, there is no doctrine, not even one guaranteed by science, which is free from infection by its context. No chasm separates science from society; any orthodoxy must be sustained by a social system, and may become the orthodoxy of that system. Yes, the natural history of man, in its modern scientific form, fills the gap left by the erosion of other great myths of creation. But I cannot see that this myth, based on the vigorous ideology of science, weighs one way or the other in the balance of power between capitalists and workers, between the U.S.A., China and the U.S.S.R. On the contrary, it raises political and economic questions which their ideologies, all of them, ignore.

And finally there is the question of man's reason, man's will and man's capacity to shape man's future, autonomously and collectively. To my mind that is a question to be resolved only in the spirit of Dr Johnson's reply to Bishop Berkeley. Free rational collective action is hard to imagine, hard to grasp intellectually. Yet man has made his own history, by harnessing the energy of nature. What has been done can be done again. Yet not without confusion, mistakes, false starts and disastrous setbacks.

I now feel free to tackle the main problems that engage men: the limits of growth and man's adaptivity in the face of limits.

In a sense the Limits of Growth controversy is a scientific controversy, but it breaks through the simple concept of natural history in each of three directions, as I hope to illustrate. It shows that the science of ecology can be transmuted readily into a philosophy or ideology; that scientific findings do not look the same to all men – what you see depends on where you stand; and that rational collective choice does not depend solely on politics, yet can be achieved only with the cooperation of those who play politics – it must be to some extent in bondage to its political environment.

In the first stage of the argument two concepts are involved:

that of a limit, and that of adaptivity. A professional would expound these to other professionals in terms of equations and curves, and this in fact is partly the method adopted in Jay Forrester's book on *World Dynamics*,[1] not the only book in the field by any means, but the one which for various reasons serves best as type case and laboratory specimen. But let me try for a plain language explanation.

A 'population' may be of men, or fish, or insects, or indeed of any artefact built to reproduce itself. Suppose two parents who have, in their short lives, one breeding season only; if they produce only one surviving off-spring the population falls catastrophically; if they produce two it remains stable, if they produce three, the population begins to increase 'exponentially'. To ease the arithmetic, say that two produce four in generation one, and the four survive to reproduce; then in generation two, four produce eight; in generation three, eight produce sixteen. The multiplication is by two in each generation, but the actual number added in each generation increases generation by generation. This is explosive growth. There can also be explosive decline, if the 'reproduction rate' (which must be carefully defined) falls below one.

This is familiar enough; animal and insect populations fluctuate very rapidly, especially if the period of reproduction is short. We shall remember for some time the proliferation of ladybirds in the very dry summer of 1976. It is equally familiar that such an increase in the rate of increase cannot continue forever. It is sustained by various inputs: *tutto si paga*, 'there is no such thing as a free lunch'.[2] And none of these inputs is infinite, not even sunlight, air and water; therefore growth cannot go on forever because eventually it hits a limit and cannot sustain itself. As it approaches a limit the rate of growth flattens and levels off. The curve climbing towards the sky bends and assumes an S-shape, the characteristic shape of the logistic curve.

But though the curve flattens it is extremely unlikely that it

1. Wright-Allen Press, Cambridge, Mass., 1971.
2. Proverbs borrowed from S. E. Finer's article, 'Big and Beautiful?', *New Society*, April 1976, p. 26.

can attain stability, either as a flat straight line ('no growth') or as a straight line slanting evenly up or down ('managed growth' or 'managed decline'). It is much more likely that there will be fluctuations round a norm, either gentle or extreme; these will depend on a number of inter-acting factors difficult to foresee and control.

There is nothing easier than to sketch on a blackboard linear increase, exponential increase, the exponential curve hitting a limit and bending like an S. The problem is to specify and to quantify. The Jay Forrester study builds up its predictions out of five 'families of curves': population, capital resources, food, non-renewable resources (of energy and industrial raw materials), pollution (a negative element in the accounting process).

This should be enough to indicate the difficulty of prediction and the scope for wrangling between rival prophets. There is guesswork about the basic data, guesswork about the shape of each curve; very complex mathematics about the interaction of five curves, which are, of course, only a few out of many, and are all themselves composite of other factors. The complexity of the calculations is not beyond the scope of big computers – but 'garbage in garbage out'. The data include hypotheses not tested and perhaps not testable in advance of experience. It is not my business here to discuss the validity of these projections, merely to state the principle and sketch the method. There cannot be exponential growth in a finite world; we have realized this, and we begin to guess at the dimensions of the problem.

And that is the basis of the problem with which I am primarily concerned, that of political adaptivity. In a sense, this is nothing new; small groups and parties of mankind have for millions of years been butting their heads against the limits of growth – by burning the forests, exhausting the soil, killing off the food animals, or (on the other side of the account) by struggling against epidemic disease or against the cold of an advancing ice age. There were many setbacks and retreats; for instance, the check to European advance into North America and the extinction of the Viking communities in Greenland. Eskimos survived where Vikings failed. Our present problems arise out of our past success. Biological selection produced the physiology of *homo sapiens*; it also gave him an astonishing and unexhausted capacity for technical, social and temperamental adaptivity. 'Man the bad weather animal'[1] has met limits, has experienced stress, has changed socially, and has survived.

So the next stage in the argument is to explain the concept of adaptivity.

I chose that word in the first instance in preference to the word 'adaptability' because I wanted to use a word with a specific technical meaning in the context of evolutionary biology. But at first I got very little encouragement from the dictionaries. The first volume of the first edition of the big Oxford dictionary, published in the 1880s, showed both 'adaptable' and 'adaptive', meaning much the same; but then 'adaptive' disappears and it is not in the first supplement nor in the shorter version of the dictionary. My old Oxford colleague, Dr C. T. Onions, had apparently joined in a conspiracy to make 'adaptive' a non-word, like an un-person. But at last I found what I wanted in the 1972 supplement.[2]

The supplement refers to the Haldane and Huxley text-book of 1927, and also to an American biologist called Osborn, writing in 1902: 'One of the essential features of divergent evolution has been termed by the writer "adaptive radiation". This term seems to express most clearly the idea of differentiation of habit in several directions from a primitive type.' This seems a very clear brief description of 'search' behaviour in the face of an obstacle or limit. Adaptivity at first involves physical plasticity: the classic Darwinian case of the Galapagos finches, differentiated in small ways to fill particular niches in the ecology of the islands, or the emergence of super-rabbits, super-rats, super-mosquitoes, super-microbes, genetically differentiated under pressure of natural selection so as to secure immunity from man-made poisons. Rabbits (as we can see on the country roads) have beaten myxomatosis and are coming back; super-rats, resistant to Warfarin, are advancing

1. Robert Ardrey, op. cit.
2. And in fact this supplement does admit one or two early biological uses from the 1850s and 1860s.

on a broad front in central England. Medical practice has always to consider the risk that if a 'wonder drug' is used extensively its pressure on microscopically small life will select out strains immune to it. Biological selection will mimic a search procedure based on trial and error and on a concentration of forces at the point of breakthrough. Man having learnt social adaptivity (as have some of the primates too) will act similarly in the face of obstacles. His search behaviour is perhaps genetically based, but it depends also on investigation, language and cooperation, which deserve such words as reason, risk-taking and courage.

I am not saying that usage always respects this rather nice intellectual distinction between adaptive and adaptable. But it is a useful distinction to sustain. A man might be adaptable individually, but his conduct might not be for the species adaptive, either genetically or socially. In other words, the adaptable person may be a chameleon, a conformist; but social adaptivity is a matter not of individual change but of social change, and that depends, other factors being equal, on the presence of an adequate supply of creative non-conformists. This is not a piece of philological whimsy: it will be recognizable at once to people versed in the semi-technical literature of leadership and management, to which I refer in Chapter 6.

The scientific problem, then, is one of adaptivity in the face of limits of growth; and it is appropriate to start from Dr W. D. Borrie's beautiful exposition of the population problem, because this has been a central issue, a crux for social biology in general, not only in the social biology of man.[1] It also has a central place in the work of Malthus, and through him in that of Darwin and Wallace, and indeed in that of Marx and Engels, by way of antipathy.

It is important to be clear that the issue called 'limits of growth' is not one of population by itself: it is always one of population in relation to resources, a relation between two curves of change over time. Insofar as the resource curve falls away from the population curve there is stress; unless something is done to ease stress by shifting one curve or the other –

1. *Population, Environment and Society*, Auckland U.P., 1973.

reduce population or increase resource – stress is intensified until there is breakdown or catastrophe. And there are various theories of catastrophe, but I had better not disgress to discuss these here.[1]

The relevant thing is that the build-up of stress involves not only two curves but many. As I explained, Jay Forrester's study of Limits of Growth builds up its composite picture out of five 'families of curves': population, capital resources, food, non-renewable resources (of energy and industrial raw materials), pollution which is incurably persistent or costly. And each of these families of curves may be disintegrated further: your family of graphs becomes increasingly complex, and your cheerful sceptic will say that at least in one key factor or a few key factors the built-in error is so large that the curve cannot usefully be plotted; or he will say that we forget the time factor and that what we shall have to face is not a simultaneous crisis on all fronts, but a succession of bottlenecks, of separate sources of stress, which can be tackled one by one; the defenders can concentrate forces, the attackers are dispersed.[2]

For the purposes of the present argument I refer to population curves only, and to that extent I over-simplify. But even to take population alone emphasizes the time factor. In all those curves there are built-in time-lags, and this is particularly important for population, because the age distribution of the population makes a great deal of difference socially and cannot be altered instantly except by extreme social measures, such as infanticide or the socially approved suicide of old people. Such measures are relatively common in human experience, extreme

1. Sir Macfarlane Burnet (*The Biology of Ageing*, Auckland U.P., 1974, p. 24) refers to 'the Hayflick limit', 'an error catastrophe, a piling up of errors, producing necessarily greater crops of new errors'; there was a brilliant B.B.C. television programme on 28 July 1975 in which Professor Zeman, Professor of Mathematics at the University of Warwick, explained in topological terms how the mathematical theory of discontinuities can be applied to 'catastrophic' change. See also C. H. Waddington, 'A Catastrophe Theory of Evolution', *The Evolution of an Evolutionist*, Edinburgh U.P., 1975.

2. Essentially these are the arguments of Herman Kahn and others, *The Next 200 Years: A Scenario for America and the World*, Associated Business Programmes, London, 1977.

cases of social adaptivity. But for practical purposes, for instance for the planning of schools and for old people's welfare, we are stuck with what we have now for a long time ahead, till a changed flow of new births changes the picture. Many things for 2000 A.D. have been settled already – barring major catastrophe. The future is already here. To quote from Bishop Joseph Butler, Mr Gladstone's patron saint, the archetype of the prudential Christian, 'Things and actions are what they are, and the consequences of them will be what they will be: why then should we desire to be deceived?'[1] Why indeed? The good Bishop seems to be saying the same as Dr Borrie said, in a striking paragraph which refers to a statistical projection postulating that India (which had in 1970 an estimated population of 576 million) will have in 2070 a population of 25,417 million. 'Obviously,' says Dr Borrie, 'this will not happen because it simply cannot happen: seven times the present world's population could not be viable in India ... This is the sort of exponential forecasting that assumes that the human species has no rational capacity for adaptation.'

'No rational capacity for adaptation' – the problem in five words. For adaptivity and rationality have hitherto belonged to separate realms of thought. Darwinism rejects final causes and purposive action, whereas rationality (unless one gives some transcendent Hegelian sense to the words reason, *logos* or *Vernunft*) – ordinary means/ends rationality, engineering rationality – requires a specification of the end before it can elucidate the means. Popper, Polanyi and others have attempted to escape from that dilemma by contrasting the universal rationality of total planning with the small-scale rationality of piece-meal social engineering – incrementalism, planning on the bottleneck, bounded rationality, the science of muddling through, and so on. Personally, I don't think the contrast helps, at least in

1. Joseph Butler (1692–1752), *Fifteen Sermons*, No. 7, S.6. It may be worth adding the next sentence: 'As we are reasonable creatures, and have any regard to ourselves, we ought to lay these things plainly and honestly before our mind, and upon this, act as you please, as you think most fit; make that choice, and prefer that course of life, which you can justify to yourselves, and which sits most easily upon your own mind.'

this context. Professor Lindblom, Professor Braybrooke and others recommend the science of muddling through as a rational procedure – most certainly they do not support any of the modern forms of anti-rationalism, irrationalism, non-rationalism. On the contrary, they think this is the way rational or reasonable men ought to behave.

The best I can do with that dilemma is to try to turn its flank by disintegrating the problem, and the case of population is a good one for the purpose. Surely three quite different but related processes are involved. First, there is the choice made at the level of the dyad, the pair of ancestors. The evidence for all periods is that a large measure of rational choice is involved in begetting and rearing children. Accidents happen: as Horace put it, 'you can throw nature out with a pitchfork, but she will always sneak back in':[1] an apt description of how that sort of decision-making works. Procreation is not always rational but it is certainly not outside the range of rational choice.

But that choice is made in the light of technology and information. If safe technologies are available for birth control and abortion, then there is no need to destroy unwanted babies, as did the ancient Greeks and ancient Maoris. The rationality of choice is bounded by the availability of information on which to base a view of the future.

Secondly, there is what the sociologists call 'collective behaviour',[2] I don't know why. In general, they mean mass behaviour of a kind which seems spontaneous, unplanned, non-rational, even self-destructive. I am not altogether happy with the sociological classification, but it serves to cover a range of phenomena which seem anomic or lawless: at one extreme, panic at the cry of FIRE in a theatre, or an outbreak of violence in the streets; at the other extreme the continuous shifting flow of fashions and of pop personalities. Of course these things can be manipulated; indeed, that is their characteristic. They do not arise out of considered choice by the participants. Either they arise in a way which seems spontaneous or they are

1. *Epistles* I, x, 24.
2. Neil Smelser, *Theory of Collective Behaviour*, Routledge & Kegan Paul, 1962.

manipulated from without by skilful and cynical advertisers and politicians.

In the case of population growth this is a matter of fashion: 'Nobody else is having large families, why should we?'

Thirdly, there are efforts at conscious social choice on behalf of a defined community. This is one view of what Bentham meant about the greatest happiness of the greatest number. Governments ought to pursue that end. Conversely, if a body which calls itself a government does not pursue that end it is not really a government but a sinister interest; indeed, if some person not called a government (Bentham, James Mill, John Stuart Mill and a lot of other busybodies) continually reasons and acts on that felicific principle he or they are to that extent assuming the role of government. What are called governments must always for their own survival play politics; but they do not particularly want to go against the general happiness principle, and there are generally self-appointed advisers at hand to play the role of Bentham and to set out a scheme of means/ends rationality. Where do we want to go, with the resources we have? How can we deploy these resources most economically in order to get there? The supposed experts may speak in fact for vested interests, or they may be totally at a loss and in hopeless disagreement. If there is a consensus of rational arguments it will carry great weight, right or wrong. Contrary to general belief, politicians do not actually prefer to do stupid things, but sometimes they have no choice, because of ignorance or uncertainty or because the demands of political survival come first.

And both these forces, ignorance and narrowness, are extremely powerful at the level at which choices have to be made for humanity as a whole.

5

The Choice of Futures

AT this point, then, I should like to turn from scientific concepts and findings to political analysis, relating the vocabulary of social adaptivity to events since the bombs went off at Hiroshima and Nagasaki thirty years ago, an obvious point from which to date the dominance of mankind and also the interdependent unity of mankind; a period in which I have, of course, been a participant, and in a tiny way a Benthamite busybody or optimizer. I think one needs to sketch the context of that period as a background to the contemporary politics of growth, but my report is very cursory and unhistorical.

First, then, there was a very swift realization among intellectuals of the meaning of the Hiroshima bomb, dropped on 6 August 1945. The movement began in the 1940s and was at its height in the 1950s; it was always an élite movement. In this case the ordinary citizen had no choice, as he or she has in population questions. But I have no doubt that the information spread by C.N.D., the Bulletin of the Atomic Scientists, and their affiliates acted as a stimulus to defiant fashions among the young. It also stimulated rational analysis, some of it public, some carried out within war departments everywhere; during that period the device of the semi-public think-tank, the RAND Corporation, was invented; it was often copied but never with such powerful effect on decision-making as in the early days of Tom Schelling and Herman Kahn.

I cannot prove it, but I am sure that the conceptual schemes then evolved greatly affected the perspective of the Cuban Missile Crisis in October 1962. To put it at the lowest, it created a common language of debate, common to White House and Kremlin, common to intellectuals inside the military establishment and to those outside it. The H-bombs of the great powers have not been de-fused, but they have been normalized or routinized.

Not so the mini-nuclears in the hands of small powers and even of guerrilla bands. That still remains to be thought through, fought through, talked through. And so does the related problem of the spread of nuclear power stations.

That period of the 1950s also had secondary effects on institutions. One of them, as I have said, was the fashion for think-tanks. And I would myself emphasize two things in which I had a tiny part: the movement for studies of the future – futurology – associated with Bertrand de Jouvenel, and the movement for General Systems Research, associated with the late Ludwig von Bertalanffy. Both of these movements survive, but I am not sure of their generalized effectiveness now that the founders have gone.

De-colonization was the other major concern of the 1950s, and in the end colonial wars in Vietnam and in Algeria traumatically affected the political cultures of France and the U.S.A. This was social learning by direct and bitter experience, affecting all classes of society; I am not sure that rational thinking played much part – France and the U.S.A. seemed to learn slowly what Britain learnt very quickly at Suez in 1956.

Then there was a phase dominated by the question – what is to take the place of colonies? The 1960s were to be the first U.N.O. Development Decade and there was a boom in the production of institutes and of text-books. When one looks at the world situation now one wonders if anything has been learnt which has practical efficacy; one can say only that the facts of the situation have been clarified. Statistics for the management of world affairs, social and economic, are still very imperfect, but they are much better than they were. Sometimes one felt that no one profited by the Development Decade except the development experts. Much effort vanished in the sands of politics and finance, and it is not surprising that the development movement generated an intellectual counter-movement, formulating in Marxist terms a theory of continuing exploitation and a new colonialism. I think myself that the theory is weak *qua* Marxism, that it has not been thought through properly in its own Marxist terms. But, speaking as an examiner, I am sure that it has quite displaced orthodox development theory from the minds of students. (I am not very sorry: André Gunder Frank at third hand has at least made a change from Talcott Parsons and Gabriel Almond at third hand.) What the next fashion will be I cannot guess. The interesting thing in the present context is the partial confrontation of the theory of neo-colonialism with the theory of the Limits of Growth.

There have been other over-lapping movements: for instance, the movement for racial equality in the United States, paralleled by the issue of coloured workers in Britain and by the anti-Apartheid movement, directed primarily against South Africa, but, in essence, introspective. My main point, however, is that the period after 1945 generated both movements and institutions, and I have given as examples the movements related to nuclear weapons, to decolonization and to economic development. All of these were weak but not worthless; a great deal could be learnt about the politics of the modern world by studying them in detail.

At the moment (1975-7) we are in the middle of a new phase, which has two aspects. One of them is that of management of money within the loosely constructed system of the so-called 'free world'.[1] The object of the game is to increase the international flow of raw materials and manufactures, and at the same time to even the balance between rich and poor countries: 'redistribution with growth', as someone has called it.[2] That is to say a movement related to the necessity for growth coexists with a movement related to limits of growth, and the latter has been sanctified, as it were, by the World Environment Year in 1972 and the World Population Year in 1973. How did that come about?

Firstly, there has been an accumulation of evidence that can properly be called scientific, even though the questions were to some extent posed from outside science. On the one hand,

1. Andrew Shonfield, Susan Strange *et al.*, *International Economic Relations of the Western World, 1959-1971: Vol. 1, Politics and Trade; Vol. 2, International Monetary Relations*, Oxford U.P., 1976.
2. Hollis Chenery and others, *Redistribution with Growth*: A Joint Study by the World Bank's Development Research Centre and the Institute of Development Studies at the University of Sussex, Oxford U.P., 1974.

though the data are still inadequate, we now know more than we ever did about human population and resources (and by 'we' I mean anyone who takes the trouble to look up standard works of reference). On the other hand, there has been sustained scientific interest in the effect of population pressure on animal populations; and indeed much scattered evidence about animal or bird territory, animal or bird aggression and hierarchy has been linked to a more general theory of animal dispersion in relation to resources.[1] And that can in turn be linked to catastrophes such as the mass migration of lemmings; to the reabsorption of the embryo in rabbits if there is overcrowding; to 'adaptive radiation' by which animals such as rats break through human defences, partly by establishing immunities genetically, partly by resourcefulness in seeking new food supplies. That is to say, we have improved data for man; we have a scientific language for population questions.

Secondly, one must remember that for at least half a century there have been quite powerful conservation groups in most Western countries, and that some of these (for instance the American National Parks Service and Federal Forest Service)[2] have penetrated government and have indeed become vested interests inside it,[3] not without enemies on both flanks. On one flank are

1. There is vigorous technical controversy about this; on one side, V. C. Wynne-Edwards, *Animal Dispersion in Relation to Social Behaviour*, Oliver & Boyd, Edinburgh, 1962 and 'Ecology and the Evolution of Social Ethics' in J. W. S. Pringle (ed.), *Biology and the Human Sciences*, Clarendon Press, 1972; on the other side, David Lack, *Population Studies of Birds*, Clarendon Press, 1966, pp. 299–312; Angus Martin, *The Last Generation: The End of Survival?*, Fontana/Collins, 1975; E. O. Wilson, *Sociobiology, the New Synthesis*, Harvard U.P., 1975, ch. 5; 'Group Selection and Altruism'; Richard Dawkins, op. cit. (p. 34, n. l).

2. There was also the I.U.P.N. (International Union for the Protection of Nature and Natural Resources) with H.Q. in Brussels (see Prof. J. T. Salena, *Heritage Destroyed: the Crisis in Scenery Preservation in New Zealand* [Reed, Wellington, 1960]. Presumably its inheritance has passed to the U.N.O. conservation agency in Nairobi.

3. A substantial bibliography of environmental politics is building up both for the U.S.A. and for the U.K., and also for the political fashion for creating 'Ministers of the Environment'. The U.K. had this in 1970, and so did New Zealand and Norway (where it is called Miliøvern). For New

those who demand production at all costs. On the left or extreme conservationist flank there were certainly 'outsiders' not coopted into government and generally regarded as a bit of a joke. Yet they are a familiar part of the scene, and certainly in the 1960s they contributed their part to shaping the 'radical chic' of student movements. They were stirred into the brew of student fashion along with anti-bomb, anti-war, anti-imperialism, anti-apartheid, and Women's Lib.

Thirdly, there are the image builders, among whom science-fiction writers played quite a notable part. One of the most reflective authors, Brian Aldiss, wrote that 'without making too large a claim for it, we may say that s.f. is the only way of dealing with ourselves as an organic part of the universe',[1] that is to say as a subject of natural history. Certainly in *The Chrysalids* John Wyndham was involved in the genetics of nuclear war as early as 1955, and from the early 1960s there were many tales (and this could be researched) of a future of fantastic overcrowding and of social adaptation, or catastrophe, or both.

But it is usual to date the existence of a specific movement to limit growth from the late Rachel Carson's book, *Silent Spring*, an enormous best-seller, published in 1962, shortly before her death. Then one can identify the appearance of the image of 'Space-Ship Earth' in a speech made by the late Adlai Stevenson to the United Nations Economic and Social Council in 1965: 'We travel together, passengers in a little space-ship, dependent on its vulnerable supplies of air and soil.'[2] He was certainly ahead of the one-man think-tank, Buckminster Fuller, who published in 1969 a book called *Operating Manual for Spaceship Earth.*[3]

Zealand my best source at present is a conference report, *Action on Environment*, dated August 1972 and issued by the Victoria University of Wellington as University Extension Publication No. 5 of 1972. See also the note on p. 72.

1. *Space, Time and Nathaniel*, New English Library, 1971, p. 11.

2. Quoted by John Maddox, *The Doomsday Syndrome*, Macmillan, 1972, p. 20. Lyndon Johnson's administration had joined the battle as early as Feb. 1966; see his message to Congress, Feb. 1966, partly reprinted as Appendix I to Robert Arvill, *Man and Environment: Crisis and the Strategy of Choice*, Penguin, 1967.

3. Southern Illinois U.P., 1969.

So far, the movement seems to have been scattered and spontaneous. At about that point it took off, and it should be possible to discover how. One aspect was the commercial exploitation of fashion as, for instance, in the B.B.C.'s television series of Doomwatch (associated with the name of Dr Kit Pedler), in many nature films, and in a flood of paperbacks.[1] Another aspect was manipulation by the international group which calls itself the Club of Rome, which was fully active by the summer of 1970. This is described officially[2] as 'a private group numbering some 75 members from many countries who have joined together to find ways to understand better the changes now occurring in the world'. This also is researchable; one could probably with a little patience secure all the names, and even some of the Club's internal papers. Certainly the names of various members of the Executive Committee have been published, and are easy to trace in the reference books. For instance, the President is an Italian, Aurelio Peccei, closely associated with Fiat and Olivetti. The Executive includes Eduard Pestel associated with Volkswagen; Hugo Thiemann of the Battelle research institute in Switzerland; an American businessman from M.I.T., who is also in some sense an international politician, Carroll Wilson; last and not least Dr Alexander King, born in Glasgow, who did a great deal when he was in the British D.S.I.R. in the 1950s to revive that rather sleepy organization and to manipulate the image of technology: he had been director of Scientific Affairs at O.E.C.D. since 1968 – and O.E.C.D., the Office of Economic Cooperation and Development, has been a rather better international think-tank than any of the subsidiaries of the United Nations.

In the summer of 1970 this group met first in Bonn, and then with Professor Jay Forrester at M.I.T. And hence the huge

1. One would need also to check the beginnings of the controversy among economists, which was crystallized in books by E. J. Mishan, *The Costs of Economic Growth*, Staples Press, 1967; and Wilfred Beckerman, *In Defence of Economic Growth*, Jonathan Cape, 1974. One must now add Fred Hirsch, *Social Limits to Growth*, Routledge & Kegan Paul, 1977.

2. Jay N. Forrester, *World Dynamics*, Wright-Allen, Cambridge, Mass., 1971, p. vii.

M.I.T. project on the Predicament of Mankind, financed by the Volkswagen Foundation and carried out by Professor Forrester and his associates.

It would be rather more difficult to trace the connections between the Club of Rome, the U.N.O., and the Environment Year; not particularly difficult to trace the travels of members of the M.I.T. team to make presentations at élite seminars and conferences; not difficult at all to trace the emergence (for instance, under our Tory government in 1970) of public organizations with the word environment or *milieu* in their titles. The research job is well within the scope of a good Ph.D. student and should be done. But there is really no doubt that at that stage the Limits of Growth movement was in the hands of an organized group trying to introduce rationality into a confused situation.

Yet the platform of the Stockholm Conference on the Environment was, in fact, fought all the way by those who spoke for poor countries against rich countries, and who treated the Club of Rome as essentially a club for rich men and rich countries. There was no breakdown, but part of the final resolution of the conference ran as follows:

The environmental policies of all states should enhance and not adversely affect the present or future development potential of developing countries, nor should they hamper the attainment of better living conditions for all, and appropriate steps should be taken by states and international organizations with a view to reaching agreement on meeting the possible national and international economic consequences resulting from the application of environmental measures.[1]

Finally, it must be remembered that this was one among several continuing quests for rationality. Into the same sequence of dates one has to fit the sophisticated international politics of Dr Kissinger in relation to the use of military force; the Yom Kippur war and the oil embargo; the continuing efforts of a less formal club of bankers and finance ministers to agree on the right tactics in a chaotic monetary situation.

1. Walter A. Rosenbaum, *The Politics of Environmental Concern*, Praeger, 1973.

Of course, I see this story from the point of view of the Western world, in which I am a participant. There are other standpoints in Moscow, Peking, the capitals of those new states which fought guerrilla wars for freedom. In all these places optimism is officially *de riguer*, and their stories are success stories, in which the heroes triumph by superior intelligence and will. What else could they say? The claim has mythological power for each of these units of action, and also a measure of historical truth. Yet the other claim, that there exists a single Marxist world-view, superior to that of the Oceanic West, has broken down in disorder, and the radical states are inexorably involved in the confused politics and economics of One World, with no greater hope that they can impose order and rationality. World politics are leaderless and autonomous, a product of chance and necessity.

And yet cheerfulness keeps creeping in. Individuals think, they create institutions, they project futures, they argue – and changes follow. In times of gloom we need the luxury of Burns's philosophy in his *Address to the De'il*:

> An' now, old *Cloots*, I ken ye're thinkin'
> A certain *Bardie's* rantin', drinkin',
> Some luckless hour will send him linkin',
> To your black pit;
> But faith! he'll turn the corner jinkin',
> An' cheat you yet.

Recent books related to biological issues in politics

Albert Somit (ed.), *Biology and Politics: Recent Explorations*, Mouton, Paris, 1976.

Peter J. Smith (ed.), *The Politics of Physical Resources*, Penguin, 1975.

Roy Gregory, *The Price of Amenity*, Macmillan, 1971.

Walter A. Rosenbaum, *The Politics of Environmental Concern*, Praegar, New York, 1973.

J. Clarence Davies, *The Politics of Pollution*, Pegasus, New York, 1970.

Richard Kimber and J. J. Richardson (eds.), *Campaigning for the Environment*, Routledge & Kegan Paul, 1974.

6

Institutions of Adaptivity

THIS pilgrimage began with the question whether the models of social biology could legitimately be applied to the social biology of man. Perhaps I did not make it sufficiently clear at the outset that I am, and always have been, looking for a valid standpoint from which to criticize and improve human institutions.

My question is not the first-level one, 'What is the right policy now, instrumentally?', but the second-level one, 'What sort of institutions will give us the best chance of choosing the right policy?' And the crux of the matter is expressed by answering, 'The right policy is to have no policy, but to act adaptively in response to an onrushing wave of events, making no commitments beyond the short range of our vision.' In three words, 'Hold your options.'

Talking in these terms I have met greatest sympathy in the first instance from students of modern organization theory. Much of this – for instance, Tom Burns's work contrasting mechanistic and organic styles of management[1] – arises out of the experience of profit-making private enterprise. But that outlook is not built into the formulation of the theory: for instance, the themes of Wilensky's *Organizational Intelligence*,[2] of Etzioni's *Active Society*[3] are equally applicable to any complex organization, public or private. The opposite state is that of the ossification or mummification of an enterprise, what

1. Tom Burns and G. M. Stalker, *The Management of Innovation*, Tavistock Institute, 1961.
2. Sub-titled '*Knowledge and Policy in Government and Industry*', Basic Books, New York, 1967.
3. Sub-titled *A Theory of Societal and Political Processes*, Free Press, New York, 1968. Compare also the difficult last chapter on 'Planning and Innovation' in J. G. March and H. A. Simon, *Organizations* (Carnegie Inst. of Tech., 1958), and a convenient synopsis of Etzioni's book in Warren Breed, *The Self-Guiding Society*, Free Press, New York, 1971.

C. Northcote Parkinson, the *Parkinson's Law* man, defines as Injelititis:

We find everywhere a type of organization (administrative, commercial or academic) in which the higher officials are plodding and dull, those less senior are active only in intrigue against each other, and the junior men are frustrated or frivolous. Little is being attempted. Nothing is being achieved. And in contemplating this sorry picture, we conclude that those in control have done their best, struggled against adversity, and have finally admitted defeat. It now appears from the results of recent investigation, that no such failure need be assumed. In a high percentage of the moribund institutions so far examined the final state of coma is something gained of set purpose and after prolonged effort. It is the result, admittedly, of a disease, but of a disease that is largely self-induced. From the first signs of the condition, the progress of the disease has been encouraged, the causes aggravated, and the symptoms welcomed. It is the disease of induced inferiority, called Injelititis. It is a commoner ailment than is often supposed, and the diagnosis is far easier than the cure.[1]

I am tempted to quote at even greater length, but that is enough to point the finger.

'Who would not weep if Atticus were he?' It would of course pass for a fair statement of the present condition of British government, by a mildly hostile critic. Insert negatives throughout, and it will serve as a statement of what I want to mean by 'institutions of adaptivity'.

Attempts to build a formal model have been traced back to the formulation of information theory in the 1940s and its application to the design of control devices, one of these industrial revolutions that happen every ten years or so at present, and one that, because of its formal power, has been as popular a source of analogies as the themes of genetic and social adaptivity. There was one notable failure in the 1950s when a great deal of American defence money was spent on an attempt to design a machine for translation from one natural human language into another. But even that failure was useful insofar as it deepened our understanding of the underlying structure of

1. *Parkinson's Law* Penguin, 1965.

human languages, and cybernetics or information theory continues to act as a linking model for the design of computers, the analysis of brain functioning and the study of very large complex systems of all kinds.

I cannot do the mathematics, and where I begin is with the prose formulations of that genuinely creative thinker, the late C. Ross Ashby.[1] The first point is this: 'The subject of regulation' [substitute 'control' if you like] 'is very wide in its applications, covering as it does most of the activity in physiology, sociology, economics, and much of the activities in almost every branch of science and life. Further, the types of regulator that exist are almost bewildering in their variety' (p. 202). This is the old problem of homeostasis; in order to persist, a complex entity must keep variations within the bounds of survival, must regulate the environment or regulate itself in relation to the environment. Secondly, 'only variety can destroy variety' (p. 207). To put it very crudely, if an enemy (the enemy may be nature) has a free choice of x tactics against you, these being independent and mutually exclusive, you are not secure against him, unless you have $x + 1$ independent countering tactics. That would (with terms better defined) give you adequate resources for complete regulation or control; lesser resources could give you partial control. This seems to me to be as applicable in Rugby football as it is in electronics or business management.

To pick a third quotation. This is about the law of Requisite Variety, and it 'says that R's capacity as a regulator cannot exceed R's capacity as a channel of communication . . .' To put it electronically, 'if noise appears in a message, the amount of noise that can be removed by a correction channel is limited to the amount of information that can be carried by that channel'. Or try it biologically: 'A certain insect has an optic nerve of a hundred fibres, each of which can carry twenty bits per second: is this sufficient to enable it to defend itself against ten distinct dangers, each of which may, or may not, independently be present in each second?' I don't know the answer, but to make sense of the question one need know only that the word 'bit' is

1. *Design for a Brain*, Chapman, 1960.

cybernetic jargon for one flip of a switch, on or off, which reduces uncertainty, goes against entropy or disorder, by the smallest conceivable amount. And there is no doubt that one can measure 'bits' passing through a channel, and the channel's maximum capacity, both for an electronic system and for a biological system. This is not soft social science but hard natural science and it is very difficult to get past Ashby's insight that these laws *must* apply to the brain, if one accepts that a brain is a physical object or machine within the realm of nature. In other words, this applies unless you refuse to accept that there exists potentially a natural history of the brain.[1] I am no judge, but it does seem that progress can be made along these lines, up to the technical limits of observation. It looks as if this ought to be homology not metaphor, science not poetry. But will it work if, as Ashby suggests, it is applied to sociology (including politics) and to economics?

I think it will clarify this if I go back to the supposed Injelititis of the post-imperial English. It is a commonplace that, in the great days of empire, art and literature, the expansion of England was a matter of individual activity not responding to a control through any single centre; I am sure this applied also to industrial enterprise everywhere and to financial enterprise in the City of London. I am not one of those who believe that the modern world has in its nature become more complex, complexity at any point of time being potentially infinite relative to the observer. What has happened, pushing this analogy, is that there are now more channels of information than there used to be, but that they tend to be arranged in a star pattern, passing through a central point or telephone exchange: that is a well-known formula for reducing the capacity of channels. One thing now seems certain, that there is not somewhere in the brain a central telephone exchange, called consciousness or the self,[2]

1. It is relevant here to refer to R. M. Young, *Mind, Brain, and Adaptation in the Nineteenth Century*, Clarendon Press, 1970; a difficult but important book.

2. David Hume in effect said this, from a different point of view, in 'On Personal Identity', *The Treatise*, book I, part IV, section VI. And see Sherrington, op. cit., throughout; and the Reith Lectures for 1976 by Colin Blakemore, *The Mechanics of the Mind*, *The Listener*, 11 Nov./16 Dec. 1976.

which monitors and manipulates all inputs and outputs.

We in Britain are in fact showing classical symptoms of over-load, with its accompaniments, stress, delayed reaction, and erratic reaction or 'hunting'. But two things I am not saying. Firstly, this has nothing to do with the distinction between public and private enterprise. The most obvious case is that of British Leyland, which simply got stuck; so did Ferranti, Rolls-Royce, Alfred Herbert, the motor-cycle industry, all of them in private hands, so-called. Secondly, it is not simply a matter of size; the common symptom has been the failure to see things which to everyone else have seemed obvious. London has been a palace of illusions. Yet, thirdly, it is hard to bring fault home to individuals.

I have seen more of top civil servants than of other top people; there is perhaps a tendency for them to block off certain areas of information from their minds, because they cannot afford to carry the overload – you can't fairly expect the Treasury man who does the N.H.S. estimates to go wandering round the grassroots of the N.H.S., sniffing its characteristic smells. But he is probably a very able and original chap, not personally lacking in initiative. Nor, fourthly, can one accuse either of the two main political parties of promoting a sort of Stalinist centralization. Perhaps it would have been better if they had, as the issues would have been more clearly stated and more easily faced. The Conservatives talk private enterprise, but politically they are primarily spokesmen of the south-east of England, the City, the big organizations and the top levels of their staff. These are not necessarily dull or stupid sections of the community, and indeed the Heath regime sought to appeal to up-and-coming young executives in finance and industry. But, in trying to speak their language, Heath lost touch with the sentiments of plain people of both parties, and he spoke recently with humility about his own failure to communicate.[1] The Labour party boasts that it stands for participatory democracy, but its members are driven by the quest for equality, fairness, justice in all things, to support in practice the ceaseless demand

1. '... but who am I to talk about communication?' Hansard, 22 July 1975, col. 347.

for central negotiation and central regulation which comes to them both from organized wage-earners and from do-gooders of all sects and sexes.

This is not an essay about British government. If it were, I suppose one would have to go back to the 1950s and even the 1930s, and one would have to risk dangerous comparisons with other countries operating on the same scale and at the same level of living standards. The criticisms entailed would not by any means all go one way.

But I am concerned at this point only with a metaphor and its validity. Is it useful (as for instance Karl Deutsch does) to interpret government in terms of flows of information? On the one hand, yes; I am inclined to think that this is the best analogy we have, and that it can take us quite a long way forward in political analysis. On the other hand, no; there is a very large gap between the flow of 'bits' in a cybernetic machine or a nervous system and the flow of communication between man and man. There are so many things about language and about non-linguistic communication between men which continue to baffle computer analysis. To my mind, the greatest of these is context; and the next is attention or salience. That is to say, the message received is never the same message as that transmitted. Something in it remains constant, the message is in some sense 'understood', since the human sender and the human receiver share a language and a situation. But no two human beings have quite the same language, quite the same concerns, the same context, however strictly they have been trained and drilled. Similarly, to each of us, in each instant, a whole universe of sensations is available, but we can attend and do attend to only a few. The focus of our attention is like a tiny pencil beam of light; what it does not light up has only a dim existence, potential not real.

This could be illustrated at length, for instance, from the transmission of messages between Americans in the hours immediately before the Japanese attack on Pearl Harbor, December 1941. But now I must take the risks involved in coming to the point. I set out with the notion of taking as a starting-point the current scientific analysis of the past, that in

78

evolutionary terms man has been a successful animal because of his exceptional resources of adaptivity; and he has been successful in a social sense, not in a genetic sense except at one remove. Social adaptation goes much faster than genetic adaptation, and it permits (within limits) the transmission of acquired characteristics. The latter is not an unmixed blessing, as we can see for instance in the transmission of ancestral hatred in Northern Ireland. But mankind so far has sustained a good working balance between flexibility and stability.

Rightly or wrongly, I went rather a long way round in reaching this question in specific terms; can that balance be sustained and if so how? What would one like to see in terms of institutions of adaptivity? and how good are the chances? Notice that I renounce prophecy about events; it is risky to prophesy about institutions, but perhaps by one level less risky. One is asking not what will happen, but what would an active society of mankind be like. The question need not be put at the level of all mankind, yet this kind of approach ought, if it is correct, to be valid at any level of a great system. There is a little book by Sir Douglas Robb, published in 1940, on medicine and health in New Zealand,[1] and it struck me forcibly when I read it that, though he did not use this language, he was setting out a programme for creating an active society for medicine and health in New Zealand.

I have been speaking in this chapter largely in terms of systems theory, the general theory of adaptivity and stability in systems. The books say that a system is a postulate rather than a thing: we postulate that such and such an aggregation of data might be regarded as a system, and we then apply an interrelated complex of concepts and propositions and see whether this helps us to make sense. As I said earlier, Karl Deutsch has been the chief agent in introducing this language into political science, and he spells out the family of words in various chapters of his text-book.[2] The words are rather different from those of systems theory in the hands of Talcott Parsons or David Easton.

1. *A Retrospect and a Prospect*, printed for the author, 1940.
2. *Politics and Government: How People Decide their Fate*, Houghton Mifflin, Boston, 1970.

The first condition is that one must be able to find a plausible boundary for the system postulated. This need not be a line, nor even a zone; it is enough to be able to say that, on the whole, things inside the system interact with one another more than with things outside the system. There is no profound difficulty in defining as systems the galaxy, the solar system, the earth/moon system, the ecosphere, the biosphere and so on, even though there are transactions across each boundary which are inputs and outputs of each system. The logical difficulties trouble us only at the level of the all-inclusive system, the universe, and of the least of all systems, and both of these beat my imagination.

The first point in this argument is that mankind can now be defined as a system. There exists also the ecosystem, the man/environment system. But (to continue a metaphor from the second chapter) man is now the dominant species, the forest canopy has closed, and the great trees create their own environment. Man is environment to man.

Secondly, can one define this as a social system? And I think the answer comes by definition: a system of men is a social system, that is an equivalence or identity. There is now a fashion for books conceived under such titles as *World Society* (John Burton),[1] *Towards a Politics of the Planet Earth* (Harold and Margaret Sprout);[2] but the titles say less than they seem to say. These are not pointers or proposals, but statements of what is by definition obvious.

Thirdly, does the social system of all mankind include a political system? This too is largely a point of definition; for most social scientists (Parsonian and Marxist alike) all social systems presently existing include a political system. The argument starts when one begins to define politics; for me it includes any decision-making for a collectivity, and then of course one has to define decision. Such a definition must include reference to will, choice and collectivity. I think it must also include communication, in the sense of interchange of information and argument. Need it also include the use of force or violence? I

1. Cambridge U.P., 1972
2. Van Nostrand Reinhold, 1971.

think it must, though I am prepared to define coercion very loosely, so that it includes withholding of benefits, unfair exchange, and even symbolic transactions which imply lowering of status and the withholding of goodwill. Yes, even in such phrases as Mama Spank; or You're a Bad Boy; or even the repressive tolerance which is the prescribed method for modern parents.

Marx of course defined his system as an arena of interactions within the white man's world as it was in his day. The modern theory of imperialism wrote in the rest of mankind by way of epicycle, and the post-colonial era has required further epicycles which blur Marx's original conception. Marx's theory was one of polarization, conflict, destruction, re-birth, and this was a plausible theory for the West in the nineteenth century. If Marxism is to continue in that vein, certainly there should be such a theory for the society of all mankind, not simply for Western bourgeois society.

One theme in these chapters has involved a tacit argument, not with Marx but with Marxism as it is taught, and as it was exemplified in a hundred or so long essays from students in two British universities which I read at the examination season of 1975. I gladly concede that the kind of functionalism used in the American analysis of development and modernization is quite dead, a casualty of the Vietnam war. I also concede that if we are to propose scenarios for a variety of imagined futures it must include among other futures a future of the Marxist type, one which foresees polarization, conflict and violent explosion as interposed between us and the promised land.

That scenario must like others be tested against the facts, and I do not think that the present facts of a plural world can be fitted to a bipolar model without distortion. And of course I do not like the picture of destructive universal conflict to which it tends. I prefer the ideology of an adaptive plural world, an active human society. But that too faces conceptual difficulties. For one thing, I am genuinely uncertain whether or not to frame a plural model functionally. I have been pursuing the biological metaphor, but it is in fact two-headed. One line of development is physiological; I do not see how one can explain the anatomy and physiology of an integrated living creature except in functional terms, but we know now how misleading it may be to transfer these concepts to the analysis of societies. I think I may be let off the hook to some extent by explaining the basic theorem of a book called *Biopolitics* by an interesting man called Morley Roberts,[1] who used the biological analogy (and indeed the analogy of cancer, which is illustrated by Sir Macfarlane Burnet's lectures) very cautiously and judiciously. What Morley Roberts suggests (e.g., pp. 17–18) is that the right biological metaphor for world society (indeed for any society) is not that of the fully developed functional structure of an animal but that of colonies of cells or protozoa which constitute very loose systems, and here he quotes Julian Huxley[2] (p. 14), in that they have 'an unstable fluctuant body' with a 'semi-permeable external membrane for defence against outsiders and a continued life with definite functions carried on by living protoplasmic units'. That is to say, there exist intermediate conditions in which we are not certain whether we are dealing with a true individual or a true system; in these situations the notion of function is heuristic only. It offers questions, not answers. Let us see how far that takes us.

If we are to look at the politics of the Planet Earth functionally, what functions can we use to classify activities? The most obvious categories are information, deliberation, execution. But one must subsume an energy function; information as order consumes little energy itself, but it never exists without carriers, and these must live. To put it crudely, the world system as it exists postulates large energy consumption, to keep men alive, to keep machines alive, to keep electronic information systems alive. I don't think that, in Marx's time, the physics existed to construe 'the forces of production' in terms of energy and its application, and we now lack even an

1. Dent, 1938. Morley Roberts (1857–1942) was a man of many parts. *Who Was Who* lists him as author of sixty-two books. Most of these were travel books and 'Boys' books', based on thirty years of wandering the world. But he edited and restored to their rightful place the novels of George Gissing, who was (like Morley Roberts) a graduate of Manchester; and he became in his sixties a serious and respected amateur in the biology of cancer.

2. *The Individual in the Animal Kingdom*, 1911.

inkling of a sociology of energy, whether as food for men or as food for machines.[1] I leave a nasty gap, noting only that events of the last four years have hammered it home that mankind is integrated by many things but perhaps above all by stocks and flows of energy under human control.

Coming back then, to communication, deliberation, execution, we find of course that fragments of this inchoate system are multi-functional. But perhaps the simplest function is that of execution, a nice ambiguous word; who is there who says 'do this or I'll shoot you'? In effect, only the authorized members of the state system, and those whom they stigmatize as criminals. The state system is a mess, as I think we all realize; one can't justify logically the fact that legitimate power to kill is in the hands of some 150 units, with populations ranging from 700 million to 150,000 or perhaps less. A state rests on a territory – no land, no state; that is not a self-evident fact of nature, but it seems now to be generally accepted as if it were. Killers who are in opposition, like the various I.R.A.s or the various Palestine guerrillas, generally legitimize themselves by a claim to territory. It is not unknown but it is unusual for killers to seek legitimacy on the basis of a landless church or brotherhood.

Action of simple necessary kinds – to check the movement of rabies for instance, to take a European case – is essentially state action.[2] But it is true that the system in which the private multinational companies are involved deploys vaster resources in money than any but a few superstates: the Russian sphere, the Chinese sphere, and who else? Perhaps not even the U.S.A., unless one labels the multi-nationals as 'American', which is not quite true. It is curious that this complex interacting system of the multi-nationals has not become an empire or a territorial state. Perhaps imperialist expansion and imperialist wars rep-

1. W. F. Cottrell, *Energy and Society: the Relations between Energy Social Change and Economic Development*, McGraw-Hill, 1955, is excellent but in detail out of date.

2. There is some very relevant material in an unpublished paper by Raymond F. Hopkins, *Global Management Networks: The Internationalization of Domestic Bureaucracies*, I.P.S.A. Conference, Edinburgh, 1976.

resented the quest for such territorial unification. But that unification failed, and we have instead of a command organization an extraordinarily complex network of command and information which would need to be studied thoroughly, in the spirit of Marx in the British Museum, before one could pontificate about the locus of power in the so-called market economy. There is no doubt that, at times, a great industrial empire can manipulate the executive state and enforce its authority by killing, as with I.T.T. in Chile; a clear case, in that the interests of one multi-national corporation prevailed over the interests of the U.S.A. as a state.[1] The fall of Allende was as disastrous for existing American policy as was defeat in Vietnam. In fact the world of money exists in parallel with the world of states, and it has different channels of information and different channels of enforcement. These are unpleasant, but I am not sure that they would be less nasty (perhaps nastier) if they were gathered into the hands of an authority corresponding to the authorities in Moscow and in Peking.

I spoke next of deliberation, and I expressly avoided talking of decision at this stage, because I wanted to keep clear of the debate about what is a decision, what is merely a happening or event. Clearly the United Nations is a deliberative body; it is not an executive body, and it is not a decision-making body in any ordinary sense of the word 'decision'. Briefly, it is not a world government; it is not likely to become one; and it would not be nice if it did.

But this is not to say that it is trivial. Conor Cruise O'Brien, in spite of his bitter experience as U.N. representative in the Congo, wrote a friendly book called *United Nations – Sacred Drama*,[2] and that metaphor is about right. Regarded as a theatre for presentations, U.N.O. holds its own. Could it be made better as a theatre? In Scotland, at least, the ladies who represented us at the World Women's Year conference in Mexico in 1975 returned appalled by ceremonial, extravagance and triviality, and I am sure their judgement was good. But

1. Anthony Sampson, *The Sovereign State: the Recent History of I.T.T.*, Hodder & Stoughton, 1973.
2. With Felix Topolski's sketches. Hutchinson, 1968.

against this one must weigh the extraordinary complex of formal and informal world organizations of which U.N.O. is titular head and grand theatre. The position is summarized by Harold and Margaret Sprout (pp. 447 ff.),[1] bless them for their pedantry. They count 2,188 non-governmental international organizations and about 200 which involve governments. Of these 200 they list 27 as constituting the U.N.O. 'family'; and it is very nearly true that the less publicized they are the more effective they are. Certainly some of them, like the World Meteorological Organization, come very near to being executive agencies, in that we all need and demand the services they provide.

I said, 'the Sprouts, bless them' because this jungle is too difficult to penetrate and assess single-handed. But to twist a phrase of Lincoln Steffens, 'I have seen the future, and it works.' There exists an enormously complex deliberative forum for all mankind, and there exist political interests and lobbyists who can get things on the agenda. But the working of this institutional network depends on communications: easy to say, not so easy to disentangle conceptually.

The first glittering generalization is that, since Sputnik and communication satellites, the world is unified in terms of voice and vision. A man can almost instantly see and talk to another man at any point of the globe. One can sit in Glasgow and watch a Test Match in Australia or New Zealand, a spacecraft launch in the U.S.A., a moon-walk 250,000 miles above our heads, the sun setting over the deserts of the red planet Mars. Miracles – but do they matter? Let us put in some reservations.

Colin Cherry, in his recent book on *World Communication: Threat or Promise?* (p. 103)[2] quotes from an article in the London *Times* of 27 July 1866 which is headed 'Shrinking World'. Yes, *1866*; the occasion was that of the first successful trans-Atlantic telegraph cable, and one expression of imperial and commercial rivalry in that period up to the First World War was a quiet commercial and technological struggle for con-

1. op. cit.
2. Wiley Inter-science, London, 1971. This is perhaps less stimulating than his earlier book, *On Human Communication*, M.I.T. Press, 1957.

trol of the world's cable network. That period ended technologically when Marconi first bridged the Atlantic without a cable in December 1901; that somewhat changed the character of the struggle for control of communications. But the big breakthrough had already been made; the submarine cables made possible instant communication within markets, instant instructions to ambassadors, instant coordination of action between executive agents anywhere in the world. It is, for example, a fairly familiar theme in history that the role of ambassadors changed almost at once: they were now held on the end of a string by Prime Ministers and Foreign Secretaries, and could no longer play the Nelson trick with the blind eye. Modern technologies have not changed the character of the breakthrough which was made a century ago.

Another glittering generalization to be treated with caution is that now there can exist, technologically, a world brain, a network of interlinked computers which contain all science in their memory stores, available for instant retrieval on demand. For a while I sat as social science representative on the advisory committee of the British Office of Scientific and Technical Information, and I duly marvelled at techniques unintelligible to me. But I kept saying my social science piece, that these machines are only a tool in the hands of scientific communities, and that the reality of unified science, the world brain, consists of groups of men and women, distributed spatially but communicating quite swiftly among themselves by techniques no more elaborate than those of books, articles, seminars and pre-prints. I suppose the big breakthroughs, like that of the Double Helix, are still generally made within face-to-face groups of what might be called 'critical mass'. But James Watson's book[1] about that episode also gives a marvellous picture of the world community of research in that field, with its strange combination of mutual sympathy and mutual animosity; indeed, with the characteristics of a global society, including what it is convenient to call a special language, because no one could possibly understand what they were saying without the sort of

1. *The Double Helix: A Personal Account of the Discovery of the Structure of D.N.A.*, Weidenfeld & Nicolson, 1968.

investment of effort that would be needed (for instance) to learn Russian.

The analogy is quite apt, for instance, in relation to the world community of some branch of mathematics, say topology. It is very nearly true to say that the essential exchange of thought between English-speaking and Russian-speaking mathematicians can take place without a word of natural language, and without using anything technically more elaborate than the postal service.

But perhaps my reservation gives the game away. The Universal Postal Union was formed in 1874, and gets no public notice except when it breaks down, which is relatively seldom. Our world brain consists not only of a very large number of dispersed technological communities but also of a framework of order run inconspicuously by quite humble technicians, clerks and messengers. In other words, I am emphasizing three interacting factors: the technology of communications, the men and women who work it in an orderly way, the élite communities which use the network as a nervous system. And this network serves not only the scientists but also the men of power, whether operating in states or in markets.

As one might expect in a world system which resembles in structure Morley Roberts's amoeba or jellyfish, a functional analysis tends to dissolve if one pushes it hard. There is of course one more aspect of communication. So far I have referred in effect to a world network of points and lines. There is also the problem of broadcast or mass communications, of words and images discharged into the air at random for anyone to capture at will. To discuss this properly would require a different metaphor or style; not only the passing of hard little 'bits' of information, but the colouring of vision by the continuous background of words, music, pictures, by the intangible atmosphere of mythology and symbolism.[1] This is a fresh topic, a very large one, and I introduce it here only to round off my original inquiry and to finish. I began with the natural history of man as socially adaptive; one way to put that

1. This is discussed more fully in my book, *Political Identity*, Penguin, 1978.

(and here I draw on a book by Edgar Dunn)[1] is in terms of the process of social learning. I don't think it is difficult to see the élite system of the world as a diffuse political system, not dissimilar in character to that of all the Hellenic city states taken together, or the Eastern Mediterranean in the time between Alexander and the Roman conquest, or the European concert of the powers as it slowly changed its pattern over 250 years. This is perhaps the world view of a Metternich, a Talleyrand, a Kissinger, perhaps a Gromyko; and such loosely constructed élite systems have not served mankind too badly in the past. But in the end they have broken; one might say, pursuing the metaphor, that they reached the end of their combined learning capacity, as did the Greek cities at the end of the fifth century B.C., the European states in the last generation before 1914. One might also say that they grew rigid because they ignored the outsiders; and the outsiders possessed force and intelligence and the capacity to innovate.

I pose therefore this final question about mass communications. We, the élite, with our TV sets and our newspapers, possess, I am sure, a new image of mankind, of a little round world which is beautiful, which is limited and which must be tended. We may not act on our image, but I am sure we have learnt it, and largely through the mass media, so thoroughly that Apollo and Soyuz were to the clever boys just a bore, bad television. But what proportion of mankind now has this image of mankind? I suspect that it is a small one, and that the requisite variety of mankind is still largely unexplored. Much is latent, therefore promising, and therefore also dangerous.

1. Edgar S. Dunn, Jr, *Economic and Social Development: A Process of Social Learning*, Johns Hopkins U.P. and Resources for the Future Inc., 1971.

Postscript

6.45 The Whole Universe Show

Eight different answers to the question *Where Do I Come From?* starting from the beginning of time.
Timesplice 8: *Shuffled Genes*
The last answer to the Big Question is the one about which scientists can be most certain.
Alan Emery, a professor of human genetics, and **Lewis Walpert,** a professor of developmental biology, appear on the Whole Universe Machine screens to explain in simple and entertaining terms the contribution that 100,000 generations of human ancestors have made to each of us. They answer the Whole Universe kids' last questions as looking back to their origins in the Big Bang, Exploding Stars, Volcanic Gases, Cambrian Seas, African Savannahs and Ice Ages they begin to see a new-born human baby through different eyes. Their guide to the Whole Universe is **Ian McNaught-Davis.**

Shown 25 August 1977

THE substance of this book was delivered as lectures in August 1975; it finally goes to press in April 1978. I have been reluctant to clutter the text with additional footnotes – but certainly the argument has not stood still.

Two divergent trends have caused me some anxiety.

Firstly, I referred in Chapter 2 to the emergence of an orthodoxy about the natural history of man. I fear that in this case (as so often in politics) an orthodoxy and a mythology go together. The inset cutting from the *Radio Times* serves to illustrate this. I hope that my exposition of the orthodoxy was so stated that it retained the character of science; that I did enough to emphasize the existence of large blanks in the story, bridged only by hypotheses and conjectures. This is unfinished science; indeed, all true science is unfinished science. But the B.B.C.'s 'scientific spectacular', addressed directly to children, stepped elegantly and recklessly over the gaps and, in the end, taught not science but a gospel story, a foundation myth.

Almost at the same time the B.B.C., in its inquiry into man's religions, 'The Long Search', took the opposite attitude to man's search for help from the supernatural; science (it is implied) has an orthodoxy which is unique, the one true faith. But all religion is relative and provisional.

In this respect the publicists of science have gone soft; it is not surprising (and this is my second point) that practising scientists have grown harder.

The ethologists, as I explained, have grown more austere (except, perhaps, for the primatologists and their talking chimps) and there have been quite sharp attacks on E. O. Wilson's book, *Sociobiology* (see p. 68, n.1), because he ventures rather tentatively into the field of human ethology.

Similarly, the geneticists insist that theirs is a hard and problematic science, that words such as 'natural selection 'and 'evolution' must be defined operationally and construed strictly. This trend[1] will reach non-specialists in Richard Dawkins's persuasive book, *The Selfish Gene*,[2] which hammers home the point that the genes have no sentiment, no teleonomy, they go on their own way as dispassionately as Lucretius' atoms; to quote Marx again, 'indestructible, impenetrable, well-armed – lacking all qualities but these; a war of all against all, the stubborn form of eternal substance, Nature without gods, gods without a world'.

This is perhaps what Dawkins would like to say, but he does

1. It goes back at least as far as G. C. Williams, *Adaptation and Natural Selection: A Critique of Some Current Evolutionary Thought*, Princeton U.P., 1966.

2. p. 34, n. 1.

not quite say it. Before the double helix was discovered, a specific piece of matter which could be identified, isolated and manipulated, 'the gene' was an instrument of thought, a postulated entity from which verifiable consequences could be deduced. Dawkins quotes a classic definition by G. C. Williams; 'A gene is defined as any portion of chromosomal material which potentially lasts for enough generations to serve as a unit of selection.' (p. 30) That is to say, the gene is, on the one hand, a piece of matter, as dead as one of Lucretius' atoms; yet, on the other hand, its scope is tested not by direct observation but by the mediating part it plays in a theory of natural selection. Dawkins is scrupulously fair in exposing the difficulties of Williams's definition, but would certainly maintain that they do not weaken his thesis.

The thesis is essentially that, by definition, there can be no gene for unselfishness or sacrifice, if these virtues also are strictly defined. Such a gene would be suicidal; would be swiftly lethal to its phenotype; and could not be transmitted. In field observation there are to be found plenty of non-human examples of apparent self-sacrifice; the existence of colonial insects such as ants, termites and bees, the very wide experience of parental self-sacrifice, the apparently suicidal behaviour of the animal which acts as sentinel in a herd and betrays itself by its outcry, or of the small birds which apparently combine to mob a predator. This mass of materials was summed up by V. C. Wynne-Edwards[1] in a book which seeks to unify it by a theory of group selection; selection for preservation of the species, not for preservation of the gene. Such selection, the 'hard men' maintain, is incompatible with the postulated machinery of genetic selection; therefore, it must be abandoned, and alternative schemes must be found to explain how a 'selfish gene' can generate behaviour which appears unselfish. Hence logical devices which are not wholly convincing, and not altogether easy to test; for instance, that the thing to be preserved is not the phenotype but the gene, and that the same gene may appear in members of a kindred, as (above all) in colonial insects.

1. *Animal Dispersion in Relation to Social Behaviour*, Oliver & Boyd, 1962.

Of necessity, this is an amateurish account of professional scientific controversy, which has the status of 'work in progress'. I refer to it here to explain why it makes one very cautious about the simple postulate that the coming of man changed the agenda: the strategy of the gene, from genetic adaptation to social adaptation.

The latter was clearly foreshadowed before man; it is not in doubt that ethology must somehow be married to genetics. There are, in many species, patterns of behaviour genetically determined, and yet there are also (in bird song, for instance) examples of behaviour which are both in-born and also plastic under the influence of social learning. I am not ashamed to treat political and social adaptivity as analogous to genetic adaptivity; but perhaps it is no more than a metaphor, a poor foundation for political science?

In that situation, I find some comfort in the position taken by Sir Peter Medawar.[1] He sets out a hierarchy of geometries, 'each a special case of the one above it'; and he goes on:

If we write down a list of empirical sciences in the order:
1. Physics
2. Chemistry
3. Biology
4. Ecology/sociology

somewhat similar considerations apply. As we go down the line, the sciences become richer and richer in their empirical content and new concepts emerge at each level which simply do not appear in the preceding science. Furthermore, it seems to be arguable that each science is a special case of the one that precedes it . . .

To pursue the analogy still further let me point out that, as we go down the list in the hierarchy of empirical sciences, every statement which is true in physics is true also in chemistry and biology and ecology and sociology. Likewise any statement that is true in biology and 'belongs' to biology is true also in sociology. Thus a characteristically physical proposition like $E = mc^2$ is true also in all the sciences below it in the list. More usually, however, a physical or chemical statement such as 'the atomic weight of potassium is 39' is simply not interesting in a subject like sociology, and does not bear at all on its distinctive problems.

1. *Studies in the Philosophy of Biology: Reduction and Related Problems*, F. J. Ayala and T. Dobzhansky (eds.), Macmillan, 1974, pp. 61–2.

This is enough to satisfy my original ambition that political science (if it is to claim scientific status) must be placed 'end-on' to the biological sciences. And I think there is a fairly rich store of viable propositions that we can slot into the space Medawar has left for us. They may indeed be 'richer in their empirical content' than those of biology. But at the same time they are looser in texture, fuzzier in outline, continuously subject to revision.

The politics of the ecosphere, which began tentatively and almost clandestinely some ten years ago, has now an established place in world politics and in state politics. There is not much doubt that ecology plays a part even in the closed politics of communist states; in Western politics it now deploys the whole text-book range of strategies and tactics. It includes, at one extreme, political enthusiasts, fanatics and do-gooders (the 'technocranks and econuts') who provide 'horse-power' for the movement. And these innocents (as is usual) may be exploited for power and profit by cooler participants whose self-interest is equally important in terms of 'energy' and 'drive'. Professor T. S. Kuhn has made familiar the phrase 'normal science'; ecopolitics is now 'normal politics', an indicator that a new dimension has been perceived and has become part of political consciousness.

In Teilhard de Chardin's phrase, 'we are "groping" ' (in French, *tâtonnement*); it is fair to give the last word to the heretic, abjured both by the Church of Rome and by the church of science:

To understand the mechanism of this revivification (in French, *reviviscence*)[1] we must return once again to the idea or symbol of 'groping' ... The fanning out of the *phylum* involves a forest of exploring antennae. And when one of them chances upon the fissure, the formula, giving access to a new compartment of life, then instead of becoming fixed or merely spreading out in monotonous variations the branch finds all its mobility once more.[2]

1. See also Charles A. Reich, *The Greening of America*, Penguin, 1971, for the use of the word 'greening', taken from the image of 'Aprilgreen' borrowed from Wallace Stevens.
2. Teilhard de Chardin, *The Phenomenon of Man*, Fontana, 1965, p. 131.

MORE ABOUT PENGUINS
AND PELICANS

Penguinews, which appears every month, contains details of all the new books issued by Penguins as they are published. From time to time it is supplemented by our stocklist which is our list of almost 5,000 titles.

A specimen copy of *Penguinews* will be sent to you free on request. Please write to Dept EP, Penguin Books Ltd, Harmondsworth, Middlesex, for your copy.

In the U.S.A.: For a complete list of books available from Penguins in the United States write to Dept CS, Penguin Books, 625 Madison Avenue, New York, New York 10022.

In Canada: For a complete list of books available from Penguins in Canada write to Penguin Books Canada Ltd, 2801 John Street, Markham, Ontario L3R 1B4.